AMAZING 2SLGBTQIA+ People in Atlantic Canada

Stories of Activism, Education, and Pride

WORDS BY REBECCA ROSE

ART BY JAMES BENTLEY

NIMBUS PUBLISHING
NIMBUS.CA

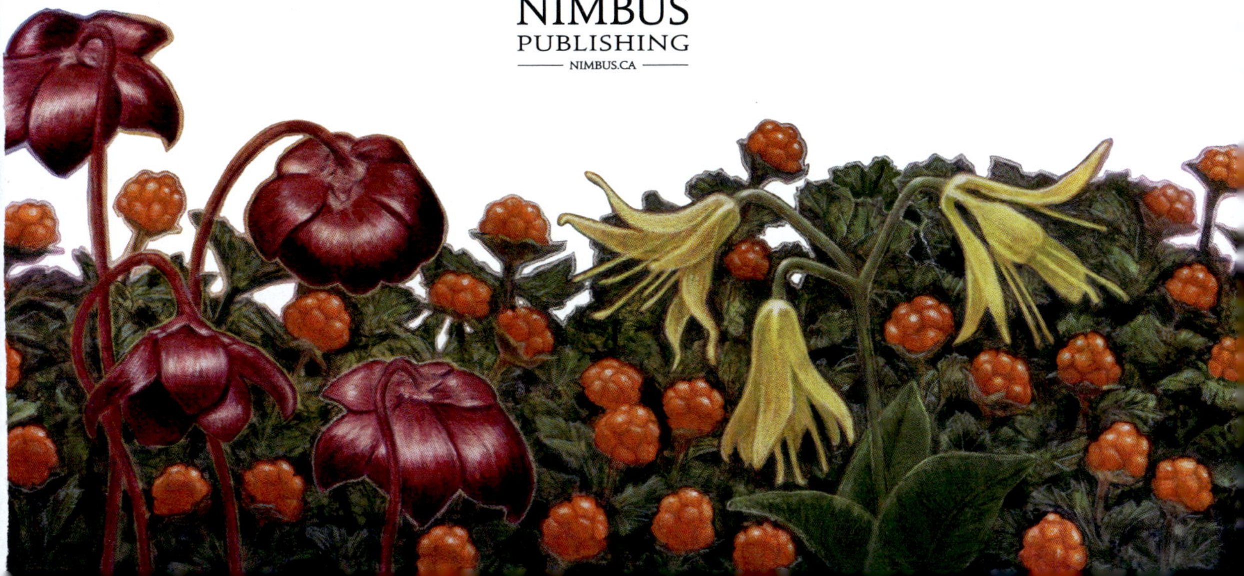

TO MY FELLOW TWO-SPIRIT, LESBIAN, GAY, BISEXUAL, TRANSGENDER, QUEER, INTERSEX, ASEXUAL PLUS (2SLGBTQIA+) COMMUNITY MEMBERS, PAST, PRESENT, AND FUTURE. WE WILL ALWAYS EXIST AND RESIST.

-R.R.

Nimbus Publishing Limited
3660 Strawberry Hill Street, Halifax, NS, B3K 5A9
(902) 455-4286 nimbus.ca
Printed and bound in Canada
NB1724
Editor: Whitney Moran
Cover design: Heather Bryan
Art direction: Heather Bryan & Claire Bennet
Interior design: Bee Stanton
Fact-checking & proofreading: Raya Morrison

Library and Archives Canada Cataloguing in Publication
Title: Amazing 2SLGBTQIA+ people in Atlantic Canada : stories of activism, education, and pride / words by Rebecca Rose ; art by James Bentley.
Names: Rose, Rebecca, 1984- author | Bentley, James, 1968- illustrator.
Description: Series statement: Amazing Atlantic Canadians | Includes index.
Identifiers: Canadiana (print) 20250335298 | Canadiana (ebook) 20250335484 | ISBN 9781774715123 (softcover) | ISBN 9781774715130 (EPUB)
Subjects: LCSH: Gay people—Atlantic Provinces—Biography—Juvenile literature. | LCSH: Transgender people—Atlantic Provinces—Biography—Juvenile literature. | LCSH: Gender-nonconforming people— Atlantic Provinces—Biography—Juvenile literature. | LCSH: Two-spirit people—Atlantic Provinces— Biography—Juvenile literature. | LCSH: Atlantic Provinces—Biography—Juvenile literature. | LCGFT: Biographies.
Classification: LCC HQ73.3.C32 A857 2026 | DDC j920.0086/609715—dc23

Canada | Canada Council for the Arts | Conseil des arts du Canada

Nimbus Publishing acknowledges the financial support for its publishing activities from the Government of Canada and the Canada Council for the Arts.

TABLE OF CONTENTS

INTRODUCTION

It's a hot Saturday in June in Kentville, Nova Scotia, and I am at the front of the Valley Pride March. I'm standing between speaker, advocate, and drag queen Chris Cochrane (aka Elle Noir) and Valley Pride organizer and drag performer Queera Bang. Before the march began, Chris and I both spoke to the group gathered before us. Me, about the history of the 2SLGBTQIA+ community in Nova Scotia, and Chris, about the importance of rural Pride events and trans representation.

As we lead the crowd into a festive parking lot at the end of the march, the DJ plays the first song Chris remembers dancing to at a gay club. Dressed in a multi-neon-coloured dress and rainbow wig, Chris waves and clacks her giant fan while Queera, dressed as Anna from the movie *Frozen*, holds a trans flag high.

This is one of my favourite memories of Pride festivities in Nova Scotia. It felt like pure joy, community, and empowerment. I hope that everyone reading this book has experienced, or someday experiences, that feeling.

In recent years, I have travelled to and spoken at many rural Pride festivals and marches, as well as schools, across Nova Scotia. I have spread the good word about the long history of 2SLGBTQIA+ community and activism in Nova Scotia from Amherst to Baddeck to Sheet Harbour to Bridgewater, and many places in between.

Meeting 2SLGBTQIA+ people from all over Nova Scotia made me think of an old saying in the queer and trans community: "We Are Everywhere." I have a vintage mug from the 1990s gifted to me by gay elder Tony Trask that features this saying atop a swirling galaxy of stars.

Originally gaining popularity in the 1970s, when lesbian, gay, and bisexual activism was on the rise, the phrase "We Are Everywhere" drew attention to the idea that queer and trans people were not the sick or bad exception to the straight (or **heterosexual**) "normal."

Gay was good (another old saying!).

We were family members, neighbours, friends, teachers, transit drivers, doctors and nurses, businesspeople, movie stars, and more. We were *people* who deserved (and still deserve) dignity, respect, acceptance, love, celebration, joy, representation, education, health care, protections, and rights. We deserved a good life. We still do.

This book proves that We Are Everywhere in the Atlantic provinces too!

The people profiled in this book come from or live in Broad Cove, Corner Brook, and Happy Valley-Goose Bay, Newfoundland and Labrador; Cape Sable Island, Eskasoni, and Windsor, Nova Scotia; Fredericton, Perth-Andover, and Saint John, New Brunswick; Charlottetown, Lennox Island, and Summerside, PEI. They come from Hong Kong, Palestine, Nigeria, Scotland, the United States, and in-between and beyond.

These folks have written plays and songs and books. They have been on TV, on the radio, and in movies. They have taught important lessons both in and out of the classroom. They have been world-renowned painters and local politicians. They preserve our 2SLGBTQIA+ histories and curate safe spaces for our communities. They entertain crowds as drag performers and athletes. They use science and activism and journalism to make things better.

There are many people I will have missed in these pages—because there are so many of us, doing amazing things! Truly living and being open about your gender and sexual identity in a world that doesn't always accept or celebrate those identities can be amazing in itself. (I have also not profiled many of the amazing folks that I included in my first book about the history of LGB community and activism in 1970s and 1980s Halifax, *Before the Parade*, to avoid too much duplication.)

By being themselves, proudly 2SLGBTQIA+, the folks in this book (and queer and trans people in general) change and expand how we think of gender and sexuality. Because of them, of us, we know that gender and sexuality are limitless and always evolving. Challenging some traditional and harmful ideas about the "right" and "wrong" ways to be, to express ourselves, to be attracted to another person, to love, to create a family (and more) makes things better for everyone!

I hope and believe that knowing there are so many ways to *just be* can make things easier when you don't see yourself represented in your immediate surroundings. When things feel confusing, unsure, unsafe, or scary.

The people in these pages are *possibility* models, because all of this and (much, much!) more is *possible* for you too.

A glossary beginning on page 131 includes definitions for the words in **bold** throughout the book.

A NOTE FROM THE AUTHOR & PUBLISHER

The author and publisher of this work are responsible only for the age-appropriateness of the content within this book, and take no responsibility for any work, or works, created or posted by the profilees outside the realm of this project.

A note on the cover: The idea for the cover was inspired by botanist Hal Hinds, who wrote *Flora of New Brunswick* about the province's native plants and was a founding member of Fredericton Lesbians and Gays (FLAG). The native flora featured on the cover was a different way to pay tribute to the 2SLGBTQIA+ community's rainbow flag. It was also a play on the saying "give them their flowers," meaning that we should celebrate people, people who often go unrecognized for their contributions. Thank you to James Bentley for bringing this vision to life.

WHAT DOES 2SLGBTQIA+* STAND FOR?

Two Spirit (2S): A term for Indigenous people. According to the Wabanaki Two-Spirit Alliance, "two-spirit" refers to "identities that exist outside **colonial** understandings of gender and sexuality." This can include Indigenous people who also identify as lesbian, gay, bisexual, transgender, queer, Indigiqueer, plus. (See the sidebar on page 120 for more on this.)

Lesbian: Women or non-binary people who are attracted to or love women romantically. (Traditionally the term has been most used by and for women. The definition has been expanded to acknowledge, in part, that lesbian identity has long included gender nonconforming people who may not identify as women.)

Gay: Someone who is attracted to or loves romantically people of the same gender as them.

Bisexual: Someone who is attracted to or loves romantically people of more than one gender. Can be shortened to "bi."

Transgender: Someone whose gender identity does not match society's expectations of the gender associated with the sex they were assigned at birth.

Queer: An umbrella term for someone who is attracted to people of the same gender, or many genders; defines their gender as being outside of binary gender norms (see the next page for a definition of "gender binary"); and/or identifies as belonging to the 2SLGBTQIA+ community (sometimes called the "rainbow community").

Intersex: An umbrella term for people born with internal and external sex traits—such as genitals, body parts, and/or body chemistry—that fall outside of the male and female binary. According to interACT, Advocates for Intersex Youth, intersex is "a natural variation in human biology, not a medical 'disorder,' and can be identified at birth, during puberty, or later in life."

Asexual: A broad identity held by people who experience (or don't experience) various levels of sexual attraction to other people.

+: The plus sign is included to cover other identities in the 2SLGBTQIA+, queer and trans, or rainbow community that are not listed in the acronym.

*This list of letters will change. It may have already changed by the time you are reading this book! That is because as we find out about new and different sexual orientations and gender identities, we add letters to the list. This makes sure that "2SLGBTQIA+" reflects the gorgeous diversity of gender and sexuality that exists and that people feel represented and included. Being able to put a name to what you are and how you feel can be empowering!

GENDER IDENTITY, GENDER BINARY, & SEXUAL ORIENTATION

Gender identity: This term refers to how you feel inside about your gender, whether you are a boy, a girl, a man, a woman, a little bit of both, neither, or more! **Gender expression** is how you outwardly present that gender.

Gender binary: The word "binary" means anything that has two parts or components. "Gender binary" is the false idea that all gender falls into either the category of girl or boy, woman or man.

Sexual orientation: Who you are interested in or attracted to romantically. Who you want to date, who you want to kiss, and who you love (as more than a friend).

If you need access to any of these definitions as you read the book, you can look them up in the glossary, beginning on page 131.

THE WORD "QUEER"

"Queer" is a word that people have a lot of different feelings about. In the beginning, "queer" meant different, strange, or weird, and was often used as an insult or slur. So, some people who grew up being called "queer" in a bad way still do not like the word.

However, in the 1980s and 1990s, some 2SLGBTQIA+ activists reclaimed the word "queer." To reclaim a word means to take a word that has a negative or hurtful meaning and use it to mean something good and empowering. The idea is that if you reclaim a word, people can't use it to hurt you. In the instance of the word "queer," reclaiming it by calling yourself "queer" means that you're saying there is nothing wrong with being different! Difference and diversity are what make humans amazing, after all.

How the word "queer" is used determines whether it can be taken in a positive, negative, or in-between way. For example, using it to make fun of someone or hurt their feelings is negative. However, if someone tells you that they are queer, and that is how they would like people to refer to their sexual orientation or gender identity, that is positive!

Some communities in the Atlantic provinces use the word "queer" to refer to an object—for example, "that queer thing over there" or "queer-a-magig"—with no connection to gender and sexuality, and that can be neutral.

A NOTE ON PRONOUNS

A pronoun is a word used to refer to a person, such as (but not limited to) he, she, or they. Both queer and trans, and non-queer and non-trans people use pronouns.

The only way to know someone's pronouns is to ask them. You can't determine someone's pronouns by how they look, dress, or sound.

Some of the people profiled in this book use more than one pronoun to reflect their (sometimes fluid or changing) gender identity and expression. In those profiles, I have alternated amongst those pronouns.

CHAPTER 1

ACTIVISM AND COMMUNITY

“*I have to have something to sing that I believe in.*”

Faith Nolan

“*I leave this life knowing my story and accomplishments have inspired others to carry on.*”

Gerard Veldhoven

“*We need to keep coming and we need to keep fighting.*”

Lee Fleming

GERARD VELDHOVEN

Born in the Netherlands, activist Gerard Veldhoven brought LGBTQ+ pride and education with him wherever he put down roots in Nova Scotia.

In 2006 Gerard and his husband, Norman Carter, hosted the first meetings of what would become the Cumberland Pride Group in their home in Amherst. Together since 1975, the couple watched Nova Scotia's first official Pride parade in Halifax in 1988. The two were married in one of Nova Scotia's first legal gay ceremonies, in 2004.

The first week of 2008's Cumberland Pride festivities included a rainbow flag–raising attended by fifty people, where Norman read aloud the Pride Week proclamation. About seventy-five people attended the next year's flag-raising. The next day, Gerard learned that someone had ripped down and slashed the flag. He was angry but did not believe it was "a reflection of the community as a whole that has been so supportive of my efforts and others

The rainbow flag was originally conceived by gay San Francisco artist and activist Gilbert Baker in the late 1970s as a symbol to represent the diversity of (what was then often called) the gay community and movement. The flag has since been updated to include more colours and symbols to represent the diversity of the 2SLGBTQIA+ community.

to bring equality for all LGBTQ+ people," as he wrote in his 2020 memoir, *A Passion for Equality*.

The first Cumberland Pride Parade was held in 2017, and Cumberland Pride honoured Gerard by naming him Pride Grand Marshall in 2018 (see the sidebar below).

After Norman's death in 2010, Gerard moved to New Glasgow, Nova Scotia, and in 2013 he was again involved in launching that town's "first full-blown Pride celebrations." The festivities, of course, included a flag-raising, for which Gerard loaned his own rainbow flag. The next year, Gerard presented the town of New Glasgow with its very own flag.

Gerard also pursued his 2SLGBTQIA+ activism by way of the written word, writing columns for *Wayves Magazine*, *New Glasgow News*, and *SaltWire News*.

"I have loved my life as an activist," Gerard wrote in *A Passion for Equality*, two years before his death in 2022. Nominated for the Order of Nova Scotia on multiple occasions, Gerard was awarded The Queen Elizabeth II Platinum Jubilee Medal in 2023.

"I leave this life knowing my story and accomplishments have inspired others to carry on," Gerard wrote in his memoirs. "To be the difference they wish to see and have the freedom to be who they are."

PRIDE GRAND MARSHALL

This special title is given to someone to recognize and honour their contributions to the 2SLGBTQIA+ community. The Pride Grand Marshall often leads the Pride parade.

FAITH NOLAN

"I'm a woman, I love women. I think men should love men." Nova Scotia–born musician Faith Nolan sings these words in the 1993 National Film Board documentary *Long Time Comin'* directed by Dionne Brand. She is performing for a crowd at a Take Back the Night march (see the sidebar on page 11) in Toronto while an ASL (American Sign Language) interpreter signs the lyrics to her song "Divide and Rule Us."

Born in Halifax, Faith is of Cape Breton/Irish, African Nova Scotian, and Mi'kmaq roots. Her family on her dad's side lived in Africville, a vibrant Black community that was forcefully relocated and bulldozed by the city of Halifax in the late 1960s. After Faith spent part of her childhood in The Nova Scotia Home for Colored Children, an orphanage for children of colour who were excluded from other orphanages, her mother moved them to Toronto.

Faith, who began playing guitar around twelve years old, started performing blues, jazz, and folk on stage at the age of fifteen! Just a year before, she **came out** as a lesbian to her mother. Faith's mother didn't respond well and threw her out of the house.

"At that time, in the queer community, we would help each other, like Black people," Faith writes in the book *Any Other Way: How Toronto Got Queer*. Faith was taken in and fed by a trans woman named DeeDee. She didn't move back to Nova Scotia until after high school.

"I started writing songs about what they call gay liberation, with a mix of black liberation and talking about Africville too," Faith told *The Toronto Star* about her early years in music.

Faith's music and her life-long social justice activism are connected. In Ontario, she founded the Kingston Women's Prisoners Choir and helped produce a documentary about women in prison called *Within These Cages*. She also worked with a group of Black Caribbean women in Toronto to create a song called "Hang On" with their **union**, CUPE.

"I have to have something to sing that I believe in. And for many years I sang songs that didn't mean anything to me, and I found myself very empty, very alone and very unconnected," Faith says in *Long Time Comin'*. "So I wanted to sing what was connected and what was true."

TAKE BACK THE NIGHT MARCH

A feminist march against gender-based and sexual violence held in cities and towns around the world. The march happens at night to demonstrate that women (and others impacted by gender-based and sexual violence) should be able to walk at night without fear of violence. For more information on gender-based violence, see the sidebar on page 85.

ERIC SMITH

Eric Smith knew he wanted to be a teacher when he was three years old. By the time he was in grade 4 or 5, he knew he was "different," or queer.

In 1987 Eric had been teaching at an elementary school in southwest Nova Scotia for nine years when the school board removed him from the classroom because he was **HIV** positive (see the sidebar on the next page). His doctor's secretary had shared that private information with the community, and some parents did not want a person with HIV teaching their children.

At that time, many people wrongfully assumed that only gay men could have HIV or AIDS. We now know that the HIV virus is spread in *some* bodily fluids, such as blood (you can't get HIV from hugging, kissing, or sharing food), and can be spread to and from someone of any gender or sexuality. We also now have treatments and tools that can prevent the spread of HIV and treat people who are HIV positive.

The parents' campaign quickly turned **anti-gay**, Eric told *SaltWire News*. Some local politicians even wanted to ban gay teachers and students from schools. Not being able to teach was "actually more scary than dealing with the HIV," Eric told the AIDS Activist History Project, as it was the only job he had ever wanted.

Because Eric had been forced to be so public with his HIV diagnosis, he was asked to be part of the Nova Scotia Taskforce on AIDS, which was studying the disease in the province. Eric knew that the taskforce, which held public meetings all over Nova Scotia, changed people's minds about HIV/AIDS for the better. By the time the taskforce finished their work, more Nova Scotians believed that people with HIV should be allowed to teach in schools.

Through it all, Eric had found another passion: making life better for people living with HIV/AIDS. He was involved in a local group called MacAIDS (Metro Area Committee on AIDS) and helped found the Nova Scotia Persons With AIDS Coalition (NSPWAC). That work gave Eric "positive, rewarding feelings," he told the AIDS Activist History Project, and a sense of accomplishment during a very difficult time. It helped him survive.

Eric Smith's efforts have been recognized with awards from the Nova Scotia Human Rights Commission and Nova Scotia Rainbow Action Project (NSRAP). He's even been the Pride Grand Marshall for Southwest Nova Pride, where it all started.

"I can look back and see that there was a big benefit to [the backlash]," Eric said when he accepted the NSRAP award, "in that it changed a lot of people's attitudes."

HIV/AIDS

"HIV" stands for Human immunodeficiency virus. According to Canadian HIV & AIDS organization CATIE "HIV can weaken a person's immune system, the body's built-in defence against disease and illness." Spread through bodily fluids shared during unprotected sexual activity or blood. Not spread through touching, kissing, sharing food or drink, sharing a toilet seat, for example. CATIE continues "with treatment and care, people with HIV can live long and healthy lives. HIV treatment also helps prevent HIV transmission to other people."

When a person with HIV is not treated medically, it can advance to AIDS (acquired immune deficiency syndrome) and result in severe sickness or death. This was more common in North America in the years before there was medical treatment (the 1980s and early 90s).

LEE FLEMING

"Twenty-five years ago, we were here at the end of a march—we didn't call it a parade—there were no floats, there wasn't much of much," said Lee Fleming. She was giving a speech after the 2019 Pride PEI Parade in Charlottetown.

"It was a human rights march," she said, referring to that march in 1994, which eventually morphed into the parade and festival. "We were fighting for our lives, it felt like, on this island. To be able to live on this island like others, without fear."

As 2019's Pride Marshall, Lee rode in a car at the front of the Pride parade. To see the excited crowds that had gathered to watch brought her to tears, she told *PNI Atlantic News*. It was so different than the atmosphere at the first march. Back then, they were afraid, but they'd had *enough* of the homophobia and *enough* of living without legal protections, Lee said in her speech. In a video series called *The Secret Social History of Gay and Lesbian PEI,* Lee spoke about how she and the others who organized that march in 1994 were amazed by the response. It was powerful.

Lee moved to Charlottetown, PEI, from Ottawa, Ontario, in 1987 after falling in love with a woman from the island at a conference the year before. Lee lived in a housing co-op with other lesbian activists, which they jokingly called Hags Haven ("hag" is a negative term for an old woman or witch, which is sometimes reclaimed by women to recognize the power of being both!). Lee and her roommates and friends organized a lesbian collective and lesbian phone line. In the mid-1980s, the collective drafted a proposal to the PEI government to protect 2SLGBQ people from **discrimination** in housing, employment, and government services.

At the time "just the word 'lesbian' would put fear and loathing into a lot of people," Lee said in her *Secret Social History* interview.

"There was no going back" after that first march, Lee told interviewer Dave Stewart. "Taking it to the streets and all of that on little PEI was probably the most radical gesture that occurred in the island's history around gay and lesbian rights," she said.

Standing on a small platform stage at the 2019 Pride festival, wearing a rainbow cap, Lee reminded attendees that 2SLGBTQIA+ rights can be taken away and there is still much to do to protect **marginalized** members of our community.

"We need to keep coming and we need to keep fighting."

COLE KIPPENHUCK

Cole Kippenhuck is an **Inuk** land and water protector (see the sidebar on the next page) from Southern Labrador, whose passion for conservation comes, in part, from growing up as a queer, two-spirit youth.

"Even at a young age, kids can be kind of cruel. So it was hard," Cole says in the docuseries *Here To Stay* on Bell Fibe TV. At the time, Cole didn't understand their gender or sexuality. They didn't feel like they were enough. "And the only place that I really found reprieve from all of the stuff that was happening internally and externally to me [was] going on the land," Cole continues. "I felt very accepted by the land and by the water."

Cole was involved in trying to stop a big dam (a structure that makes electricity from fast-moving water) at the Muskrat Falls waterfall in Labrador. The community, near Happy Valley-Goose Bay, was scared that the flooding needed to make the project happen would damage the local environment and wildlife as well as the wild food people relied upon.

"...We told them our safety is being threatened—we're at risk of being poisoned, at risk of being drowned, and we no longer feel safe in our communities because there's a lot of outsiders here telling us that their work and their lives are more valuable than ours," Cole told *The Independent* news.

Cole has also worked in the community sector since 2001 and has their own business, Crow Kinship Consulting, which helps groups "grow their practices, **decolonize** their policies, and expand their understanding of **intersectionality** and diversity."

Cole left Labrador at age sixteen, but now credits moving back with saving their life. Cole's mother survived **residential school**, and Cole worked hard to heal from **intergenerational trauma**. Though they struggled with **addiction**, deepening their connections to their Inuk culture made them feel whole.

Having come out as a butch lesbian (see the sidebar on page 18) at eighteen, Cole now views their gender, sexuality, and relationships as more fluid. Always shifting, changing, and growing.

LAND AND WATER PROTECTORS

The term "land protector" or "land defender" (or "water protector"/"water defender") is used by and for Indigenous people taking action to prevent harm to land, water, and the wildlife and people who live there. In doing so, they are also often fighting to preserve traditional ways of life and sacred sites and practices.

During a conversation hosted by the National Centre for Truth and Reconciliation, Cole described identifying as two-spirit, **genderfluid**, or **pansexual** this way:

"I'm going back to the ways that I would have known my ancestors to be which is not needing to define gender or my relationship structures or my sexuality.

"I just…I am. I am."

BUTCH & FEMME

Butch: A word used to describe a queer person with a more masculine gender identity and expression. This can include demonstrating behaviours and interests that are considered more masculine or dressing or cutting your hair in what is considered a more masculine way. It has special importance to lesbian or queer women and can be used to push back against expectations that women or people assigned female at birth 'should' be feminine.

Historically, butch women were often paired with femme (or feminine) women in "butch/femme" romantic couples. (Though butches can also be coupled with other butches or people who do not identify as either.) There are all different kinds of butches.

Femme: A word used to describe a queer person with a more feminine gender identity and expression. This can include demonstrating behaviours and interests that are considered more feminine, dressing in what is considered a feminine way, or wearing makeup and jewellery. It has special importance to lesbian or queer women and can be a way to push back against the expectation that queer or lesbian women are 'supposed' to be more masculine.

Historically, femme women were often paired with butch (or masculine) women in "butch/femme" romantic couples. (Though femmes can also be coupled with other femmes or people who do not identify as either.) There are all different kinds of femmes.

AMY PARSONS

As a Black, deaf, queer woman, the concept of "nothing about us without us" drives much of Amy Parsons' work and activism. Often used within the movement for disability justice, this phrase means that no decision should be made about a group of people *without* the people who will be impacted by that decision.

"My activism is focused on First Voice/lived experience and shining the light on hyper-underrepresented groups," Amy writes in an email. This means shining a light on other people who, like Amy, are members of various marginalized communities and who do not often hold positions of power in society.

Of both African Nova Scotian and Irish decent, Amy was born in Halifax, Nova Scotia (Kjipuktuk), but her family has deep roots in the Black communities of Lucasville and Weymouth Falls. Amy started school at age four with day classes for Deaf children and later moved to mainstream public schools with an American Sign Language (ASL) interpreter.

Passionate about language and educational justice, Amy has worked as the associate director for interpreting services at Gallaudet University, the world's only university serving Deaf and hard of hearing students, and with Deaf and hard of hearing students with the Atlantic Provinces Special Education Authority. She has also worked with the Government of Nova Scotia to offer input on how they can better support people with disabilities.

In 2017 Amy was part of a **grassroots** group of people with disabilities who brought attention to problems with a law that was meant to improve access for people with disabilities. (Access can mean being able to physically enter a space; get information in a way that works for you, such as Braille or sign language; get the services you need to live a dignified life, and more.) Presenting to lawmakers, Amy stressed that the law should "not [be] drafted by people who don't have the lived experience." The group was able to help make improvements to the law and "beautifully characterizes" the type of change-making Amy wants to be involved in going forward, she writes.

In 2025 Amy followed her "love of history, activism and research/writing" into the public administration graduate program at Gallaudet University. Completing this degree will allow Amy to continue to help making government **policies** that better serve people with disabilities.

There are many people who create the laws, policies, and services that impact people with disabilities that say, "'We would love to, but we can't [make things truly inclusive],'" Amy writes. "I believe we can."

FIRST VOICE

This term refers to someone who has experienced something for themselves. That is, someone who has lived that experience, also known as "having lived experience." For example, someone who has experience being unhoused would be considered a first voice when discussing solutions to homelessness.

ANDREW JANTZEN

When queer and multi-gender (see the sidebar on page 23) disability advocate Andrew Jantzen witnesses injustice, he just has to do *something*. Often that something is speaking up—whether it be online, in the media, or going directly to the people in power.

"My hope is by me saying something, other people around me also say something," Andrew explains.

Andrew first came out as queer after moving to Antigonish, Nova Scotia, from Alberta to attend Saint Francis Xavier University in 2006. Within a week of being on campus, Andrew met other queer and trans people and thought, this "seems like me." Unfortunately, shortly thereafter Andrew's dorm room door was vandalized with **homophobic** graffiti. That incident partially motivated them to get involved in the campus 2SLGBTQIA+ group, X-Pride.

At St.FX, Andrew pushed the school to respect people's pronouns in official communications and on their degree and helped organize a drag show, Priscilla: Queen of the Highlands. Together with Kinnon Ross MacKinnon, Andrew created Rainbow Warriors, a support and social group for queer and trans youth in the Antigonish area. Later, Andrew took their 2SLGBTQIA+ activism even farther. They joined the Board for the Nova Scotia Rainbow Action Project and a group that convinced the Nova Scotia government to fund (some) gender-affirming health care (see the sidebar on page 31).

In his mid-twenties Andrew began to use a cane, and in his late twenties, a motorized wheelchair due to a loss of mobility from two different medical conditions. His disability impacted his life "drastically." Eventually they needed assistance from a personal care worker to do crucial things such as eat and bathe. He couldn't work, attend school, or socialize.

Again, Andrew advocated. For better home care, for more accessible spaces and events, and for people with disabilities to be able to live good lives. He's worked for a group that makes assistive devices for people with disabilities and as an accessibility specialist for the government, and in 2022 was awarded a Queen Elizabeth II's Platinum Jubilee Medal for his efforts.

In a fundraising video Andrew made with friends to pay for an important surgery, he says he's "just trying to do whatever I can to improve the way things are in our province for people like me and people who are not like me too."

MULTI-GENDER

This term refers to having multiple gender identities, sometimes at the same time, and sometimes at different times or depending on the setting. This means that multi-gender people can alternate amongst pronouns.

KY REES

In 2024 Ky Rees travelled to Cape Town, South Africa, to attend a conference of 2SLGBTQIA+ activists from around the world. The International Lesbian, Gay, Bisexual, Trans and Intersex Association (ILGA) World Conference's aim was to plan the fight against homophobic and **transphobic** hate and violence.

Originally from Newfoundland and Labrador, Ky was one of about 1,400 attendees at the conference. A passionate labour activist, they were there on behalf of Unifor, a labour union in which Ky has held several leadership positions, specifically representing the queer and trans community.

Unions have a history of fighting for 2SLGBTQIA+ rights, and Ky's activism adds to that legacy. They've run trans education training sessions for fellow union members, pushed for employers to recognize non-binary gender markers and helped individual workers socially transition (see the sidebar on page 26) in their workplaces.

LABOUR UNION

A labour union is an organization created by workers to fight for good/safe working conditions, fair pay, and benefits such as health insurance.

Ky's drive to work on behalf of 2SLGBTQIA+ workers comes from the understanding that how much money someone has or doesn't have (known as their "social class" or simply, "class") can make someone's life either much easier or harder. People who face oppression, such as 2SLGBTQIA+ people, **BIPOC** folks, and people with disabilities, can make less money due to discrimination. Ky believes that we have to address oppression based on class and identity together in order to achieve true justice.

Ky's activism has made a big impact. Back in 2014 Ky took Newfoundland and Labrador's provincial government to court to ensure that people's government IDs reflect their true gender, not the sex they were assigned at birth. At the time, Newfoundlanders and Labradorians couldn't change the "male" or "female" marker (see the sidebar on page 26) on their IDs unless they had surgery to change their reproductive organs and/or genitals. There was no gender marker that represented people who didn't identify as men or women, but as something in-between, both, or none of the above.

That meant that when a person presented their ID, the gender marker on it could conflict with how that person expressed their gender. For example, if you were wrongly identified as a boy at birth but identify as a woman, that would mean sharing with anyone who looks at your ID that you are transgender. You'd have to decide "whether or not you want to out yourself and have to have a discussion then and there about the reason this doesn't match is because of X, Y, or Z," Ky said at the time. These types of situations can cause stress for trans and non-binary folks and can even be a safety risk if the person checking the ID is transphobic and decides to become violent.

Because of Ky's legal challenge, the government of Newfoundland and Labrador changed the law to allow people to change their IDs to reflect their gender identity without surgeries. "[I'm] overwhelmed, but in such a good way," Ky told the CBC after learning of the decision.

The fight, they said, wasn't just for them, it was "for all trans people."

GENDER MARKERS

The letter (such as M for male, F for female, or X for non-binary or other) on someone's official documents or identification (ID) that indicates their sex or gender.

SOCIAL TRANSITION

The term "social transition" refers to when a trans or gender diverse person changes outward expressions of their gender, such as their name, pronouns, clothing and other aspects of their appearance, what bathroom they use, and more.

CHAPTER II

INCREASING REPRESENTATION

"How can you know who you are if you don't know where you come from?"

Dave Stewart

"All my life, I've been struggling not to be pushed into a box."

Candy Palmater

"I love that I am trans. And I love that I am queer. And the more I hold myself close and fully embrace who I am, the more I dream, the more my heart grows and the more I thrive."

Elliot Page

TOMMY SEXTON

In vintage footage of the *CODCO* sketch comedy show on CBC Television, cast member Tommy Sexton sings a made-up song to a fake crowd: "I am a homo, h-o-m-o m-a-n. I'll say it again." ("Homo" is short for "homosexual," or gay.)

This early 1990s skit, one of Tommy's last, was one of the many times that the proud gay man played gay on TV. Representation was especially important during this era, when there were fewer positive depictions of 2SLGBTQIA+ people. "At a time when performers were often urged to hide their sexuality, and gay men were usually the subject of punchlines instead of the ones delivering them, Sexton made sure that would never be the case on *CODCO*," writes Andrew Sampson to the CBC. The author of the soon-to-be-published book *Tommy Sexton Superstar* continued, describing how Tommy used this rare opportunity, appearing regularly on TV across the country, "to further **the gay agenda** at every opportunity."

Born in St. John's, Newfoundland, in 1957, Tommy left school to pursue acting in grade 10. "I think he was born to be an actor, I really do," Tommy's mother, Sarah Sexton, said in the documentary *Tommy...A Family Portrait*. She remembered Tommy's childhood love for dress-up and high heels. Classmates teased Tommy, calling him a "fairy," which was a negative name for gay.

But the joke was on them. Tommy co-created the CODCO comedy troupe in 1973, using his lived experience as a gay man to write and star in skits that Canadians loved. In the early 1980s, he appeared on Newfoundland's televisions as part of another sketch comedy show, *The Wonderful Grand Band*, and by 1986, when the CBC began to air *CODCO*, he was on televisions across Canada.

"It's hard to really understand just how beloved Tommy would have been then. He was a household name. When people saw Tommy on the street, they would go up to him and ask for an autograph," Andrew Sampson told author Rhea Rollmann in her book, *A Queer History of Newfoundland*. "This well-known public figure was sort of exposing everyday people to what it looked like to be a gay person in the province."

Tommy died in 1993 at thirty-six years old from complications due to AIDS. Tommy's mother, Sarah, became an HIV/AIDS activist after his death. Today there is a short-term housing project in St. John's for people living with or at risk of HIV, named The Tommy Sexton Centre.

"May his memory remind us never to be stingy with our understanding and our compassion," Sarah Sexton told the CBC in 2006.

ALLISON BREWER

Allison Brewer wears a Hawaiian shirt, and her short grey hair peaks out from under a wide-brimmed pink hat trimmed with a matching feather boa. Draped in a rainbow sash, she holds a large rainbow umbrella.

It is 2010 and Allison is the Grand Marshall for Fredericton, New Brunswick's first ever Pride parade.

As for what it means? "It's great," Allison tells NB Media Co-Op interviewer Charles LeBlanc with a smile. "It means that Fredericton has come a long way."

As a founding member of the Fredericton Lesbians and Gays (FLAG) group in 1980, Allison has seen a lot of change. The group organized gay and lesbian dances, a magazine, and a phone line for LGB people who needed information or support. If a woman called the phone line, she was referred directly to Allison.

"I think there is a real need here," Allison said of New Brunswick in an interview with Tom Warner in 1993. "We don't have the resources that say Toronto would have, and so people seem to work a whole lot harder and get a whole lot more involved than in a larger centre where it feels as though things are being done for you."

In 1995 Allison represented national 2SLGBTQIA+ group Egale Canada at the United Nations World Conference on Women in Beijing, China. After holding up a *Lesbian rights are human rights* banner, Allison was shortly detained by United Nations authorities.

Back in her hometown of Fredericton, Allison was elected the leader of the New Brunswick New Democratic Party (NDP) in 2005.

A mother of three, today Allison and her son Will, who live in Nova Scotia, are both fierce advocates for people with Down syndrome.

As a member of the LGBT seniors group the Elderberries, Allison was interviewed by Global News in 2024 about the rise in anti-queer and anti-trans hate. A self-proclaimed "Lesbian Tomboy," Allison had gender-affirming top surgery at the age of sixty-eight (see the sidebar below.)

Allison told the interviewer that many in the rainbow community had become comfortable over the years, given the victories and rights we have won. "We have to stay vigilant," she urged.

GENDER-AFFIRMING HEALTH CARE

This term refers to health care that supports and nurtures someone's gender identity. It can include but is not limited to medical professionals who understand and respect diverse gender identities, medications and hormones, mental health supports, and surgeries that help someone's body feel in line with their gender. Some, but not all, trans and gender diverse people undergo these treatments.

GERRY ROGERS

Gerry Rogers was the first openly gay or lesbian person elected to Newfoundland and Labrador's provincial legislature and the first to lead a provincial political party (see the sidebar on page 34 for more on this.)

"I was very out when I ran," Gerry says of her first election. "I did that because I think it was so important for our youth." At the ceremony where Gerry was officially made an MHA (Member of the House of Assembly), she wore a pink triangle and stood "as tall as I possibly could," to demonstrate her pride.

Born in Corner Brook, Newfoundland and Labrador, Gerry represented the people of St. John's Centre in the legislature for eight years and was the leader of the provincial New Democratic Party (NDP) for ten months. When she left elected life, she told the CBC that one of the things she was proudest of was the victories she helped shepherd in for transgender people, such as having provincial health care pay for gender-affirming surgeries.

"Human rights, our human rights—myself as a woman, myself as a lesbian—our rights are never given to us," Rogers told the CBC. "They're hard won, and we often have to push and push and push for them."

Gerry knows first-hand what it's like to be an activist fighting for change. She was a founding member of the lesbian advocacy group Newfoundland Amazon Network, or NAN. (Amazons were a group of all-women warriors in Ancient Greek stories.) Gerry recalls in *A Queer History of Newfoundland* that there "were no activities specifically for lesbians. So a bunch of us decided: well let's start a group." Gerry had previously lived in Montreal, where she made documentary films with the women's National Film Board studio, and had been an activist for people living with HIV/AIDS.

NAN and Gerry were involved in helping to pass a provincial law to protect gay, lesbian, bisexual, and queer people from discrimination. The Newfoundland government finally—after twenty years of community pressure!—changed the Human Rights Code to do just that in 1997.

Gerry is still creating space for 2SLGBTQIA+ people in Newfoundland and Labrador, now in rural Newfoundland! One of about thirty lesbians who lived and vacationed in "old Bay houses" in Broad Cove over the course of thirty years, Gerry helped organize "Come Home Queer" weekends in the community. (Gerry's partner of over thirty years, Peg Norman, came up with the name.)

Queering Newfoundland and Labrador Tourism's "Come Home Year," which asked locals to come home to visit, this event asked speakers to share their stories of being 2SLGBTQIA+ in the province. The event was a huge success, accompanied by music from acts such as Kellie Loder and much gaiety (which means fun!).

"It's busting myths, you know? Rural Newfoundland and Labrador is not backwards," Rogers told the CBC. "There are lots of people here now who have children or grandchildren or relatives or friends, people in their own community, who are queer. And there is acceptance."

PINK TRIANGLE

The pink triangle was a symbol originally used by the Nazis in World War Two to identify gay men, who they imprisoned in concentration camps for being gay. (Lesbians were sometimes given black triangles.) It has since been reclaimed by some in the 2SLGBTQIA+ community as a symbol of empowerment and pride.

PROVINCIAL LEGISLATURE

The provincial legislature is the place where elected representatives (politicians) make laws and decide how much money goes into provincial government services such as education and health care. This can also be known as House of Assembly or Legislative Assembly.

PROVINCIAL POLITICAL PARTY

A provincial political party is a group of people who have similar ideas around how to run the provincial government, what kinds of laws it should have, and what kinds of services it should offer. Political parties support specific people to run in elections, who ask the public to vote for them to work in the provincial legislature (see sidebar above). Examples of provincial political parties in Canada are Green, Liberal, NDP, and Progressive Conservative.

DAVE STEWART

Dave Stewart began documenting the history of gay and lesbian life on Prince Edward Island on film after he spoke to some young people who weren't aware of this history.

"I realized our history was disappearing," he told the *Eastern Graphic.* As Dave told the CBC a few years earlier: someone had to preserve PEI's gay and lesbian histories, so why not him?

The result was an interview series on YouTube, *The Secret Social History of Gay and Lesbian PEI,* co-produced by Laura Chapin. Dave interviewed seven people, including Lee Fleming (see her profile on page 14)! In total, Dave spent seven years uncovering and documenting these **undertold** histories, with Laura's help in the seventh year.

Dave had an inkling that he might be gay as a young boy in the 1970s and 1980s. And he knew he should hide it, because those around him may not accept his queerness. He didn't have any gay role models growing up on PEI. By the time he was a preteen, he got good at "acting straight" by mimicking the boys around him. But hiding that part of him hurt.

"When society tells you you don't have a place in it, you turn that inside and you hate yourself," Dave told host Cynthia King on *The Belong Podcast.*

That's another reason why Dave created *The Secret Social History of Gay and Lesbian PEI,* to ensure that younger queer islanders could see themselves in older queer islanders.

"Visibility is crucial not just for the community, but the public at large just to know what their world is," Dave told the *Eastern Graphic.* "[The world is] not just one thing, it's made up of many different types of people."

Dave's second "talkumentary," *POSITIVE: When HIV/AIDS Hit PEI*, premiered on December 1, 2022, World AIDS Day. It features interviews with two gay men diagnosed with HIV in the 1990s and a cousin of Allan Hickox (the first person to openly die of AIDS on PEI, in 1987). The community's and church's negative reaction to Allan's HIV/AIDS really impacted Dave, keeping him **in the closet** longer.

Dave received an award from the PEI Museum & Heritage Foundation for his history work in 2022 and a City of Charlottetown Heritage Day Award in 2023. Most importantly, he knows that (queer) history can tell us so much about where we are and where we are going. As he told the *Eastern Graphic*: "How can you know who you are if you don't know where you come from?"

CANDY PALMATER

Candy Palmater spent her entire life pushing back against other people's ideas of who and what she could and should be.

"All my life, I've been struggling not to be pushed into a box," Candy told *Xtra Magazine* in 2008. "I'm not fully straight, but I'm not fully gay. I'm not fully Mi'kmaq, but I'm not white. I'm an athlete and I'm really girly in how I present…I just don't fit into boxes. I am what I am."

Candy was many things. In her 2022 memoir, *Running Down a Dream*, Candy described herself as a "queer, Indigenous, recovered-lawyer-turned-feminist comic who was raised by bikers in the wilds of northern New Brunswick."

The great-grandchild of the last hereditary chief in Ugpi'ganjig (Eel River Bar), Candy grew up in nearby Point La Nim. Of her seven siblings, Candy was the second to graduate high school. After leaving her studies at St. Thomas University, Candy moved to the biggest city in the Atlantic region: Halifax, Nova Scotia.

"There was a deep yearning in me to break free," Candy writes in her memoir. "...I had decided I was going to push the boundaries of my life and see what existed out there on the sharp edges."

An academic rock star, Candy graduated at the top of her Dalhousie Law class. But she soon discovered that a career in corporate law didn't suit her. What Candy really wanted was her own TV show, and she told everyone about her idea for *The Candy Show.*

When Candy was thirty-nine, the Aboriginal People's TV Network (APTN) picked up her lively talk show, which would run for five seasons. It ushered in many opportunities for the charismatic Candy, including hosting her own show on CBC Radio, a recurring guest co-host spot on CTV's *The Social*, and roles on the TV shows *Trailer Park Boys* and *Run the Burbs.*

Candy was supported by her manager, and wife of twenty years, Denise, who "has been picking up my slack as I continue to run down this dream," Candy writes in her memoir.

She loved heavy metal music and was adorned in tattoos. She was an anti-racist and feminist activist. She was diagnosed with osteoarthritis at age thirty-eight, had a hip replaced at forty, and used a cane.

Candy passed away at the age of fifty-three, leaving behind a legacy of self-acceptance and doing good.

As she told *Xtra*: "When you pull all the politics away, kindness is what it's about."

OSSIE MICHELIN

In May 2025 Ossie Michelin's second documentary, *Feather Fall*, premiered in the gymnasium of the old school in Elsipogtog, New Brunswick.

The National Film Board (NFB) film details this Mi'kmaw community's struggle to stop an American company from fracking on their land and the viral photo that Ossie took in 2013 of the resistance. (Fracking is a dangerous method of pumping the ground to release gas and shale deposits. It can pollute waterways, harm wildlife, and even increase the chance of earthquakes.) The powerful photo was of a Mi'kmaw woman, Amanda Polchies, kneeling in prayer, holding an eagle feather over her head in front of a line of RCMP officers, who were there to end the protest.

Four hours after Ossie tweeted the picture, it had been shared thousands of times.

As a journalist for APTN, Ossie said, "I knew the non-Indigenous perspective would be there in the news already, but it was my role as an Indigenous journalist to make sure the community and their allies were fairly portrayed."

That photo of Amanda, called *Mi'kmaq Woman, 2013*, has since come to represent Indigenous resistance. It was even named the best photograph in the Canadian Museum of Human Rights' 2017 seventy-photo exhibit, *Points of View.*

Ossie grew up in North West River, Labrador, surrounded by their Inuit culture. Their mother is a settler nurse from Ontario, and their dad's side of the family in Labrador is Inuit. Upon moving to Montreal to study journalism, Ossie found a general lack of knowledge about Labrador.

They've been telling Indigenous peoples' stories ever since.

"Our stories make us human; they are how we pass on culture, language and ways of life," he told the CBC. "They're how we connect with our families and ancestors. When you remove us from our own stories, we lose who we are."

As a freelance journalist, Ossie does a little bit of everything. His first documentary, *Evan's Drum*, which documents a mother and son's shared passion for Labrador Inuit drum dancing, debuted in 2021. Just a year later, Ossie achieved a childhood dream when he was selected to work with National Geographic Society's Pristine Seas on a documentary about Nunatsiavut (see the sidebar below). He's even directed a podcast for the CBC, *Telling Our Twisted Histories*, which works to **decolonize** words that have impacted Indigenous Peoples.

But at the core of it all is this: "Indigenous people are still here, we're active parts of society," Ossie says in a video for Concordia University. "And our history is happening with you and alongside you all at the same time."

NUNATSIAVUT

Nunatsiavut is the Inuit region of Northern Labrador. It is the homeland of the Labrador Inuit.

ANDREW LAM

It's funny, but journalist Andrew Lam didn't like writing in high school. It wasn't until she began studying journalism at the University of King's College in Halifax, Nova Scotia, that she realized she does enjoy the process. That is, when she's writing about topics she's interested in.

As a proud member of the queer and trans community, Andrew is most passionate about reporting stories that impact 2SLGBTQIA+ and other marginalized communities, as well as working people (these are sometimes called "labour stories").

"I think it just comes down to caring about other people and my community," they say.

Andrew's identities as a queer and trans Chinese person give them the "courage to push for fair and equal coverage of people in my communities," who are often missing in news coverage.

Born in Toronto, Andrew grew up both there and Hong Kong. She was working in banking when she first thought to pursue journalism as a career.

It was during the beginning of the Covid-19 pandemic, and Andrew was inspired by the news stories that told important truths and helped the public understand what was going on.

In 2023 Andrew began working for the CBC in Nova Scotia. In the summer of 2025, they celebrated their one-hundredth published story with the national broadcaster. (Ever a journalist, they track all of their stories in a spreadsheet.) It's especially impressive knowing that Andrew wasn't confident they could make it as a journalist when they started in the field. "Sometimes though," Andrew says, "doing things outside your comfort zone is good."

Having pushed through that uncertainty, Andrew has been able to draw much-needed attention to stories that impact not only the communities she's a member of, but all Nova Scotians: the local impacts of **climate change**, efforts to increase access to gender-affirming care for queer and trans people, the affordable housing crisis, the struggle for accessibility for people with disabilities, and more.

What makes Andrew most proud, though, is the attention they brought to acts of anti-2SLGBTQIA+ vandalism targeting queer- and trans-run businesses in Halifax as well as the impact of the rising costs of living on workers.

As she writes on her website, Andrew's journalism aims to reflect "the full diversity of where we live."

JENNIFER CRAWFORD

When Jennifer Crawford won the reality TV show *MasterChef Canada* in 2019, they knew exactly what they needed to do: move home to rural Nova Scotia.

It was there that Jennifer first dreamt up their pastel-hued alter-ego, Moon Miss, named for the iconic East Coast ice cream. Much like queerness, Moon Mist's combo of banana, grape, and bubble gum is "different." It's also beautiful and delicious.

Moon Miss, "an extraterrestrial ethereal being," soon became Jennifer's persona as a pro wrestler.

Yes, a pro wrestler.

In the ring, Moon Miss superkicked, flipped, and body-slammed their way to victory in 2022, winning the UCW (Ultimate Championship Wrestling) Atlantic Canadian championship belt.

As a child growing up in Kingston, Nova Scotia, Jennifer was in love with pro wrestling. It was "so beautiful and so pretty, so masculine and so feminine all at once somehow," they said in their 2023 CBC documentary, *Bump and Feed*. This combination spoke to Jennifer, a rural queer kid who "didn't always understand what was in my heart" or "have the vocabulary to speak about my gender, about my sexuality," they added.

That understanding and language came when Jennifer recovered from an addiction to alcohol while living in Toronto. Being **sober** helped Jennifer "get back to that kid that I was, the one who didn't quite know why I didn't fit in, in spite of my very best attempts." For now, they've settled on the term "non-binary" (see the sidebar on the next page) to describe their gender identity, but that may change.

Cooking filled Jennifer's time when they quit drinking. "Food is something that not only keeps me well but helped me to get well when things were really tough for me," they said in a video for Xtra.ca.

Nestled in the Nova Scotian woods, Jennifer continues to nurture their love of food: growing and preserving, baking challah (a braided Jewish bread), and cooking in their wood stove. Each week, on the eve of Shabbat, the Jewish day of rest, Jennifer lovingly prepares their challah, meditating on the faith's concept of world repair. Deeply committed to freedom for the Palestinian people, Jennifer channels that feeling into initiatives such as the Challah for Ceasefire fundraiser.

In 2024 Moon Miss took a break from wrestling, due to a lack of Covid-19 safety precautions.

Jennifer hopes to "one day fade into local lore as that autistic queer who once won a reality show, then became a pro wrestler, then quit it all" to fight for justice, cherish nature, and spend time with their beloved animal and human pals.

NON-BINARY

"Non-binary" is a gender identity that exists outside of the man/woman gender binary (see page 4). Someone who is non-binary can identify in a variety of ways, including a mix of man and woman/masculine and feminine, somewhere in the middle, or neither. It can also include people who identify as genderfluid, genderqueer, and more. Non-binary people sometimes refer to themselves as "enby."

NEURODIVERGENCE

A way people's brains work that is considered different than the way that other people's brains typically learn, process information, and function. Neurodivergence is not a disorder. Just like being queer (a word that originally meant 'different'), there is nothing wrong with being neurodivergent! It's a term that helps us understand that brains can operate in many different ways. Some examples of neurodivergence include autism, ADHD, and dyslexia.

ELLIOT PAGE

Dressed casually in a black long-sleeved T-shirt, jeans, and sneakers, and sporting cropped brown hair, actor Elliot Page stares directly into the camera, self-assured.

The photograph, by trans photographer Wynne Neilly, was the first of an (out) transgender man to grace *TIME* magazine's cover. (The cover of *TIME* magazine is kind of a big deal and has also featured the likes of Billie Eilish, Taylor Swift, and Barack Obama.)

Though it was acting that made Elliot famous, his public announcement that he was trans made him an icon for trans and queer people around the world. "Hi friends," began the 2020 Instagram post. "I want to share with you that I am trans." Having already come out as queer during a high-profile speech in 2014, the 2020 post announced his name, identity, and pronouns. Though new to the general public, Elliot first truly acknowledged his trans identity about four years earlier, around his thirtieth birthday.

"I love that I am trans. And I love that I am queer," the post continued. "And the more I hold myself close and fully embrace who I am, the more I dream, the more my heart grows and the more I thrive." Announcing that he was trans, Elliot told *Them* magazine, gave him "a surge of energy, creativity, inspiration, and true joy in creation."

A point of pride for many trans and queer Nova Scotians is the fact that Elliot, likely the most well-known trans guy in the world, is also from the province. North End Halifax to be exact.

Growing up, some of Elliot's earliest memories were of not relating to the gender he was told he was: female. He would ask his mom if maybe one day he could be a boy.

Elliot's mother did not react well when Elliot first told her he was queer in his twenties. However, in an interview with Sam Smith on their podcast *The Pink House*, Elliot said his mother was "happy and supportive" when he told her he was trans years later. "She's gone through her journey," he added.

A professional actor by the age of ten, Elliot starred in 1997's award-winning TV movie *Pit Pony*, set in Glace Bay, Nova Scotia. The rest of the world got to know Elliot in his role as a pregnant teen in the indie movie *Juno*, released to great acclaim in 2007. Afterwards, the intense pressure from the film industry to present as feminine was painfully uncomfortable for Elliot.

As an actor, Elliot has played roles in big productions such as several X-Men movies, *Whip It*, and Netflix's superhero show *The Umbrella Academy*. As an activist, Elliot directed the documentary *There's Something in the Water*, based on a book by Dr. Ingrid Waldron, about environmental racism (see the sidebar on page 48) in Nova Scotia. He also advocates against laws that discriminate against trans people and for life-saving services such as gender-affirming health care (see the sidebar on page 31).

Elliot published his memoir, *Pageboy*, in 2023, which details the process of realizing and accepting his queer and trans identity. He wrote the book in a cabin in the woods in Nova Scotia. Upon the release of his memoir,

ENVIRONMENTAL RACISM

The term "environmental racism" refers to when governments and businesses make decisions that expose Indigenous, Black, and other racialized communities to increased pollution and toxins. This can include things like placing garbage dumps near these communities, allowing facilities (such as factories and plants) to put toxins into the environment and water near these communities, not cleaning up after these polluting industries, not providing clean water (including for drinking) to these communities, and more.

Elliot wrote on Instagram: "I hope that by sharing my journey it can help demonstrate that we all—queer, trans and anyone who supports the basic human dignity to live authentically—will not be silenced."

ASHLEY MCKENZIE

Cape Breton, Nova Scotia (Unama'ki)–based filmmaker Ashley McKenzie has long found herself "on the outside of things."

"My desire to tell cinematic stories has always been tied up with feeling like an outlier," they say. "I felt a strangeness in my artistic sensibility, regionalism, and queerness—probably in that order. As they explain on their website, these things—being queer and living and making art on an island on the eastern edge of Canada—led her to telling stories that "may otherwise be overlooked."

Ashley's films centre on fellow outsiders, people who don't fit society's narrow ideas about what is normal or acceptable. The people who are left out or treated poorly due to their differences, their hardships.

The two main characters in her first feature film, *Werewolf*, struggle to recover from drug addiction in a small Cape Breton community. In *Queens of the Qing* (pronounced *ching*) *Dynasty*, Ashley follows the budding friendship between an island teenager hospitalized following a mental health crisis and a student from Shanghai who volunteers at that hospital.

"They're in a world that doesn't really value them," Ashley told *Xtra* of the two characters, Star and An. "But when they spend time together, it's like they're creating their own space that allows them to expand out from the [limits of the] everyday world." Just as queer and trans people have done for thousands of years. "I feel free," An says while playing a virtual reality game with Star in the movie.

Both films have been shown at film festivals near and far, including in Berlin, Germany, and have earned multiple awards for best film and best writer/director.

Queens of the Qing Dynasty gently explores both gender and sexual identity. While An, played and co-created by Ziyin Zheng (pronounced *Tze-ing Jung*), never commits to a label, their gender and sexuality is suggested to be queer. Almost in passing, Star tells An she is asexual (see the sidebar below), an identity she shares with Ashley who is on the asexual spectrum. (In this case, "spectrum" means a range or variety of related identities.)

"I always felt a bit mismatched or broken until realizing there is such a vast spectrum of experiences that can exist within the ace umbrella," Ashley says.

Originally from New Waterford, Cape Breton, Ashley and her partner, artist Sig Burwash, have firmly rooted themselves in Cape North. In a world where most films are made in large cities, Ashley is committed to making films in and about Cape Breton, an act that is in itself queer. It may be challenging, but it is true to who Ashley is as a person and an artist.

"It will get too complicated if I start thinking about what other people wanna see," they told Halifax weekly newspaper *The Coast*. "How do you even make artwork if that's on your mind?"

ASEXUAL

Asexual (or "ace") identity acknowledges that people experience different and changing levels of physical (sexual) attraction to other people throughout their life. Some people experience no physical attraction to others, and that's okay, while others may experience intellectual, emotional, and touch attractions (to name a few) more powerful than sexual desire.

CHAPTER III

DOING DRAG

“*Anyone can do drag, that's what makes it so special.*”

Barbra Wire

“*Just be who you want to be. And don't let nobody stand in your way. If they do, just keep doing what you're doing.*”

Scott Thompson, on Jerry States

“*If there is somebody sitting watching that might be struggling with something, with their own identity, they can look at me and hear my message and know that it's OK.*”

Normand Hector, aka Normani

JERRY STATES

Jerry States was a teenager when he started doing drag (see the sidebar on the next page) in late 1970s Halifax.

At the time, there was no legal protection against anti-gay discrimination. Homosexuality had been considered a mental illness until 1973. Halifax's Gay Alliance for Equality (GAE) was founded in 1972, and in 1976 the alliance opened its own bar and social space called The Turret.

Born in 1961 in Windsor, Nova Scotia, Jerry, who was African Nova Scotian, later moved with his family to Mulgrave Park in Halifax. Jerry's former partner, Scott Thompson, an African Nova Scotian gay man from Amherst, Nova Scotia, recalls that the shy Jerry figured out his sexuality by hanging out with his friends Travis and Peenee, who were "openly gay and quite happy." Jerry became "pretty adventurous and...quite jovial," says Scott, who officially met Jerry and his friends at The Turret.

"He held his head up high," Scott said about the strong-willed Jerry.

DOING DRAG

When someone outwardly expresses, plays with, or performs (usually an exaggerated or queer version of) gender and sexuality, it is referred to as "doing drag." This often involves wearing costumes, wigs, makeup, and/or jewellery. Drag can be performed anywhere—whether it's to music on stage, in other venues such as drag story time, or via social media, to name a few. Drag is considered a form of self-expression and an art form; sometimes it can be someone's job.

People who do drag can call themselves "drag queens" (a feminine expression of gender), "drag kings" (a masculine expression of gender), or "drag performers" (a more gender-neutral or flexible expression of gender). Anyone can do any kind of drag.

"When we went out, he didn't care if anybody said anything to him or not. You know, sometimes he would get upset and get a little emotional, but he kept on."

"*That's just me, who I am*," Scott says of Jerry's attitude. "*You either love me or don't love me*."

Jerry, Travis, and Peenee started doing drag at Scott's house, where they would get ready to go downtown. Scott would put on soul music and the trio would perform. Eventually they moved their act to the bars, where sometimes Scott would rap as Blowfly, and the queens would be his backup dancers. Jerry chose the drag name Marchand, and sometimes the three would perform as Nunya and Her Business. Jerry sewed Marchand's outfits, and used his own hair (which he wore in an afro out of drag). He fashioned

Marchand after Black American singers Natalie Cole and Melba Moore, using his own voice to sing their songs. That is, until Whitney Houston came along. "Then it was all about Whitney," Scott says with a laugh.

Jerry loved drag and continued to perform after he moved to Toronto in the early 1980s. Scott and Jerry lived together until Jerry passed away of AIDS-related complications in 1993. In the last few months of his life, Jerry would still dress in drag around the house.

Jerry States's legacy, says Scott, is drag and "just be who you want to be. And don't let nobody stand in your way. If they do, just keep on doing what you're doing."

NORMAND HECTOR, AKA NORMANI

Whether giving presentations as Normand or performing in drag as Normani, Normand Hector is the Black queer example they didn't have growing up in the 1980s.

"I always want to make sure that I leave a positive message," Normand told *Southwest Magazine*. "That if there is somebody sitting watching that might be struggling with something, with their own identity, they can look at me and hear my message and know that it's OK. You can embrace who you are and just move forward."

Born and raised in Saint John, New Brunswick, Normand was one of eight siblings. Though their mother taught them to stand tall no matter what, Normand didn't know where to turn while sorting out their Black, queer identity. Bullying made Normand uncomfortable to play sports, wear what they wanted, or even attend prom (their biggest high school regret).

A past provincial government's decision to get rid of protections for trans and gender diverse students brought Normand back to the time when they felt uncomfortable in their own skin.

"I just think of the things I missed because of the fear factor, because I was afraid to live, and I was afraid to live because I didn't have the support," Normand told *BlackLantic Podcast.*

Today, Normand stands in their truth in front of some large, and maybe surprising, audiences.

Normand first donned drag to entertain their mother, who they were caring for with their husband, Richard. (Married for over thirty years, Normand told *BlackLantic* that Richard was "a tremendous support" and the love of their life.) They took Normani online in 2018 and performed their first show a year later.

Drag is more than dressing up as another gender, Normand told ByBlacks.com. "It's creativity, it's the exploration of oneself, it's great entertainment..."

Normani has since dazzled audiences at Saint John Sea Dogs hockey games and the 2022 Memorial Cup (which was televised on TSN), to name just two! Hockey Canada and Hockey New Brunswick both hired Normand to present to coaches and players about respect and creating safer hockey spaces, including as the keynote speaker at Hockey Canada's Beyond the Boards summit.

Still living in Saint John, "there's not a day that I don't wake up and thank the powers that be above for the opportunities that I've been presented and this life that I'm living," they told *BlackLantic.*

In 2026 Normani announced they were stepping away from drag to explore making an impact in other ways, writing:

"New Brunswick, you raised me in resilience and wrapped me in community. From small stages to big moments, drag taught me that even here, especially here, we belong. I leave the spotlight with gratitude, knowing the courage we built together will keep shining in every town, every heart, every brave step forward. Keep showing up. Keep making space. I love you."

CHRIS CATHERINE COCHRANE, AKA ELLE NOIR

Growing up in 1980s Glace Bay, Cape Breton, Chris Catherine Cochrane didn't know the word "transgender." Today, Chris, who affectionately describes herself as a "tranma" (a trans grandma), is a Black, trans educator, advocate, and agitator.

"Everything that I do in drag, out of drag, activism, is for an eleven-year-old little boy named Christopher William Cochrane who didn't have anybody to talk to, didn't have anything to look to," Chris told *PNI Atlantic* news. "So I want to make sure that the generation that's coming up behind me doesn't have to worry about things like that."

In 2025 Chris celebrated twenty years performing as celebrated drag queen Elle Noir. Her drag persona came to be when nineteen-year-old Chris donned drag as a dare and later competed at a famed local talent show. Drag allowed Chris to be herself, and she soon felt more comfortable in drag than out of it. It was in therapy that Chris first heard the term "trans" and learned about the act of **transitioning**. It wasn't until living in Toronto that she first saw other trans women who were performing drag. It made her think that maybe she could be both a drag queen *and* a trans woman.

"Through that I found that I was more outgoing and a lot less afraid of the world as Elle Noir," Chris told Halifax newspaper *The Coast.*

Since leaving the navy, Chris has worked as a makeup artist, at the Youth Project (see the sidebar on page 58), with Halifax Pride, and speaks and performs clear across the Atlantic provinces. She has won many drag pageants as well as awards. Chris has also become a beacon for other queer and trans people who want to live unapologetically as themselves, especially youth.

In 2019 Chris was marching in Truro's Pride parade, draped in the pastel blue, pink, and white of the trans flag, when she heard a small voice from the crowd: "I'm trans too!" It was a young Black girl, and this was the first time she had acknowledged her trans identity in public. Seeing an adult who looked like her gave her the confidence to speak up.

"We're not only fighting for these kids to be able to be themselves," Chris says in a Dartmouth Heritage Museum video. "We're fighting for these kids to be able to have a future."

THE YOUTH PROJECT

The Youth Project is a group in Nova Scotia that works to "make Nova Scotia a safer, healthier, and happier place for 2SLGBTQIA+ youth—through support, education, resource expansion, and community development," according to their website, **youthproject.ns.ca**.

JASON DESILVA-SPURRELL, AKA ROUGE FATALE

Legendary Nova Scotian drag queen Rouge Fatale, known as Jason DeSilva-Spurrell out of drag, is a drag mother to around twenty drag children (see the sidebar on page 60). On Mother's Day, Jason's Facebook wall is peppered with well wishes from these kings, queens, and in-betweens.

"It is the best way to pass down the traditions and the history," they say of being a drag mother. "It is how we have [done so] for eons." Rouge herself was mothered by Nova Scotian queen Deva Station, the drag persona of Steven MacLeod.

Born and raised in Glace Bay, Cape Breton, Jason first came out as bisexual at age seventeen in the late 1990s and then later as gay. Self-described as a queen with "a heart as big as her mouth," Rouge made her drag debut in the 2002 Miss Gay Sydney Pageant.

Jason's grandfather was a member of The Men of the Deeps, a choir of current and former miners who often backed Cape Breton singing superstar Rita MacNeil. As Rouge, Jason performed at Glace Bay's Savoy Theatre, as her grandfather had done before her.

Rouge has performed on stages across Canada, hosted CBC radio's afternoon show *Mainstreet* and the Halifax Pride Parade TV broadcast and was the first-ever drag queen to read to kids as part of Halifax Pride's Fabulous Fantastic Storytime. A former daycare worker, Jason, as Rouge, showcased books that reflect different types of families, gender identities, and expressions, such as *And Tango Makes Three* and *Morris Micklewhite and the Tangerine Dress.*

"I think it's super important…that kids can actually see that being part of the LGBTQ community isn't something they have to hide away from," Rouge told CBC Radio of that first drag story time in 2016. "This is just opening up more doors and showing the kids that it's perfectly fine to be gay or lesbian or queer in this community and in this province." Today, Jason delightfully identifies as "queer as all get-out."

Having won the title of *The Coast*'s Best Drag Performer ten times, Rouge was retired from the category and entered into the paper's Best of Halifax Hall of Fame.

After more than two decades as Mama Rouge, drag continues to be Jason's passion.

"Drag has brought me the greatest thing you can get in this world, life experiences! The things I have gotten to do because of Rouge!"

DRAG MOTHER OR PARENT

A "drag mother" or "drag parent" refers to a more experienced drag performer who mentors newer drag queens, kings, and gender diverse performers. Those newer drag performers are known as their "drag children."

ANNABELLE BABINEAU, AKA BARBRA WIRE

Drag queen Barbra Wire sits in a yellow plastic chair in a classroom as two young children approach. Wearing a large curly yellow wig and purple eyeshadow, she is dressed in a mauve lace and sequin outfit that looks like a figure skating costume.

Barbra greets the children with a smile: "My name's Barb. What's your name?" The sweet interaction is part of CBC's video *Queens and kids in class: An honest conversation about drag, gender and dress-up*, which features Barb and fellow drag queen Rose Beef.

One child pipes up: "Are one of you a girl and one of you a boy?"

"I am a girl in real life," Barbra responds. "But anyone can do drag; that's what makes it so special."

Annabelle began dressing up and performing elaborate recitals for her parents in their living room when she was just a wee child. She just didn't know drag was a thing, and a thing she could do. "The thought of having me as a kid seeing something like this on that stage—I think it would have helped me a lot growing up," they told the St. Thomas University student newspaper *The Aquinian*. Attending school in Moncton, New Brunswick, Annabelle (who today identifies as bisexual) was never exposed to positive representations of 2SLGBTQIA+ people and culture, only insults and slurs. Bullied, Annabelle found comfort in books.

It was her grandmother who taught a young Annabelle to knit while watching TV together. Annabelle's passion for performing and textile arts ("grandma crafts," they call them) combined to create their unique style of drag. Wearing a wide array of whimsical and brightly coloured crocheted, knit, and quilted hand-crafted costumes, Barbra declares on her website that she brings the "same energy as your Acadian aunt who loves to dance in kitchens." Gracing stages and drag story times throughout the Maritimes, she especially loves visiting those in rural Acadian communities.

The confidence Annabelle drew from Barbra helped them make the transition to being a full-time artist. They explore the overlaps between their Acadian/Chiac (see the sidebar below) and queer culture, using rug tufting, quilting, embroidery, and even film.

Like identifying as queer, an artist is just who Annabelle *is*.

"We are just simply that, artists. And we're just doing art," Annabelle said of drag performers in the docuseries *Under the Wig*. "And if you take the time to look at our art, you'll find that it's steeped in joy and acceptance and kindness."

"Sometimes we do like to push the envelope, but usually it's because we have something to say," they add.

CHIAC

Chiac (pronounced *shee-ack*) is a blend of Acadian French, English, and some Maritime-specific slang that is primarily spoken in southeastern New Brunswick. "Chiac" is also a word used to describe the unique culture of the Acadian communities with roots in southeastern New Brunswick who speak it. Chiac resists both French and English language "rules." It can also be spelled "chiak" or "chiaque."

TANAS SYLLIBOY, AKA ANITA LANDBACK

On March 24, 2024, drag performer Anita LandBack of Eskasoni First Nation stood beside John R. Sylliboy of the Wabanaki Two-Spirit Alliance on the stage of the biggest music awards show in Canada: the Junos. They wore a handmade corseted black-and-red leg-baring gown. Their earrings were by Neve's Beadwork, also of Eskasoni First Nation.

"John R. and I are both 'living with two-spirits.' In the English language, this is known as two-spirit," Antia said in Mi'kmaw. ("Ni'n aq John R. Etuijijaqamijuinu'k, aqalasie'wiktuk telui'tmek 'two spirited.'") "We lead this resurgence as we speak our language in Mi'kma'ki, Wabanaki, or the Land of the Dawn," they exclaimed in English to great applause. Tanas Sylliboy (Anita's name out of drag) and John R. Sylliboy worked with Mi'kmaw Elders to develop a Mi'kmaw word for the term "two-spirit."

This was a historic moment and a full-circle one for Tanas. When Tanas witnessed Indigenous actor Lily Gladstone open their Golden Globe acceptance speech in the Blackfoot language, they posted on Instagram the next day that they "had this profound feeling of pride that our languages are being heard and seen and celebrated." The post continued: "And I thought, one day I want to have that opportunity to do that for Mi'kmaq, to do this for us." Anita's own appearance on the Junos came just two months after Gladstone's speech.

Tanas uses the Mi'kmaw gender-neutral "nekm" as one of their pronouns. They told the CBC's *Canada's A Drag* they picked the drag name Anita LandBack because it was "unapologetically Indigenous." Land Back is an Indigenous movement to get Indigenous lands, which were stolen through colonization, back into Indigenous control.

A nurse practitioner who went on to medical school, Tanas started doing drag after moving to Halifax, Nova Scotia (Kjipuktuk), and not feeling seen,

THE WABANAKI

Wabanaki Two-Spirit Alliance is "a collective of Two-Spirit, Indigiqueer, LGBTQQIA+ kin, Elders, Knowledge Carriers, youth and allies from Wabanaki territory and across Turtle Island. We advocate for and celebrate 2SLGBTQQIA+ communities through relationship-building, 2S-led research, and community-led initiatives" (w2sa.ca).

Wabanaki territory includes the territories of the Mi'kmaq, Wolastoqiyik, Passamaquoddy, Abenaki, and Penobscot Nations and spans eastern Québec to Newfoundland, Labrador, Nova Scotia, Prince Edward Island, New Brunswick, and the state of Maine.

they said in a Moose Hide campaign video. Anita made her triumphant debut at a queer and trans BIPOC Halloween drag show organized by Elle Noir and Mya Foxx.

In 2025 Tanas was presented the Candy Palmater Award by Halifax Pride, which celebrates the "life, enthusiasm, talent, and intelligence that flowed through all of Candy's work, and to foster these same qualities in others."

"Anita's this love letter that I have for who I am as Mi'kmaq, who I am as a Two-Spirit person, and who I am on a day-to-day basis whether or not I'm in scrubs or I'm in heels," Tanas told the CBC.

XÉNIA GOULD

In spring of 2025, at the Éclat de Fierté Gala in Dieppe, Xénia Gould was named the "Acadian queer artist who has made the most impact outside of New Brunswick." She accepted the award virtually, from her adopted home of Montréal.

Starting in 2017, Xénia began to identify the parts of her Acadian culture that also felt queer, working them into her art. The award was the culmination of ten years of being publicly and proudly queer, Acadian, and creative. "For me, the word 'queer' was the word that guided me at the beginning of my artistic practice," she said in her speech.

Today's Acadians descend from those who survived the Acadian Expulsion, either evading capture by British soldiers or later returning from far-off places (see the sidebar on the next page). For hundreds of years, Acadians have resisted attempts to destroy their language and culture, revelling in what makes them unique. They are, as Xénia says in the CBC docuseries *Canada's A Drag*, "a society of French-speaking rebels in Atlantic Canada." That spirit of rebellion is also central to queer and trans identity, community, and culture.

These similarities extend to the language that Xénia, and many Acadian New Brunswickers, speak, Chiac. "Chiac is the queerest language of them all," she told the *Mount Allison Record*. "When we talk about queerness, it is not just about being gay, it is challenging norms in a way and if you look at Chiac, that is what it is—taking parts of English and taking parts of French and creating this other thing..."

Xénia first brought queer Acadian culture to the masses with her YouTube character, Jass-Sainte Bourque: an undeniably queer, moose-hunting, camouflage-loving, rural-living, Chiac-speaking vlogger. Later, she took on the drag persona of Chiquita Mére, a happily divorced Acadian auntie who lip-synchs traditional folk songs. In 2019 she co-organized Moncton's first Drag Ball.

A comedian, drag performer, poet, actor, and playwright, Xénia is a very "multi" multi-disciplinary artist. In 2023 Xénia published her first book of poetry, *des fleurs comme moi* (*Flowers Like Me*), and in 2025 she premiered her one-woman play, *Juste Vide Ton Coeur* (*Just Empty Your Heart*).

Her art, grounded in self-expression, guided her to her **transfeminine** identity.

As a queer Acadian artist, the possibilities are limitless. "I think mashing those two identities together allows for like an endless well of inspiration," she says in *Canada's A Drag*. "You can take anything out of Acadian culture and ask yourself what would that look like if it were queer. And then all of a sudden you get to create something that has never been created."

THE ACADIAN EXPULSION

In the mid-1700s, the British violently deported over eleven thousand French people from what is now Nova Scotia. At the time, Acadians had been living in what was called Acadia, or Acadie, for over 150 years. Refusing to swear allegiance to Britain, they were forcibly expelled from the province. Those who survived the voyage by boat were taken to parts of what is now called the United States (especially Louisiana, which led to Cajun culture and identity) or parts of Europe. This event is also known as le Grand dérangement.

CHAPTER IV

CREATING SPACE

"When you get to go and shine light into places that don't have a lot of queer representation, it's a gift to do that."

Jeremy Dutcher

"There's something really powerful in being seen and feeling heard and feeling understood, and I think that I represent that for people."

Carly "CJ" Jackson

"My responsibility is to pave the road that someone else is going to travel."

Robert Wright

ANDREA CURRIE

When Andrea Currie won an Atlantic Book Award for her first book, *Finding Otipemisiwak: The People Who Own Themselves*, her child Rowan was by her side.

Adopted by a white family at birth in Winnipeg, Manitoba, Andrea didn't learn that she was Red River Métis (see the sidebar on page 70) until she was thirty-eight. "All of a sudden everything made sense," Andrea said on the CBC's *The Sunday Magazine*. "Who I am made sense."

Andrea had left her childhood home, one that she describes as unhealthy and unbearable, at age seventeen, eventually arriving in Halifax, Nova Scotia (Kjipuktuk). It was there, in her early twenties, that Andrea came out, first as lesbian. Since then, she has identified as bisexual, two-spirit, and more recently, queer and **Indigiqueer**.

The year after finding her birth family back on their homeland in southern Manitoba, Andrea's child, Rowan, was born. Rowan's Métis grandmother flew to Kjipuktuk to be there for the birth. This was an important step in the family's healing from the intergenerational impact of the Sixties Scoop (see the sidebar on page 70). Rowan would never have "to live one minute without knowing who they are," Andrea writes in *Finding Otipemisiwak*.

While *Finding Otipemisiwak* is Andrea's first book, she has been writing poetry, prose, and songs for a long time. In the 1980s, Andrea joined the Afrocentric a cappella singing quartet Four the Moment. Among many performances over a period of over twenty years, the group opened for renowned author Maya Angelou, revolutionary activist Angela Davis,

RED RIVER MÉTIS

The Red River Métis are the descendants of First Nations People and European (primarily French and English) settlers who created unique community, culture, values, traditions, language, and more. "Our People have a strong distinct identity and share a common history in the great western plains centered in the Red River Valley that is entirely our own…Red River Settlement—now Winnipeg—is the birthplace of the Métis Nation and the heart of the Métis Nation Homeland." (Manitoba Métis Federation, **mmf.mb.ca**)

The Red River Métis also have a proud history of resisting colonization, which is when a foreign country tries to take over and control lands that are not theirs and the people living there.

THE SIXTIES SCOOP

A government effort to separate Indigenous children from their families, culture, and land and assimilate them into white, settler culture through adoption. A continuation of the residential school system.

and won the 2022 Polaris Music Heritage Prize for their album *We're Still Standing*.

For the past three decades, Andrea has worked as a psychotherapist, including as a community-based therapist in We'koqma'q First Nation in Cape Breton (Unama'ki). Andrea is committed to providing healing for survivors of the residential school system and Sixties Scoop, and their descendants. She also spends as much time as possible with her Métis culture, family, and ancestors, travelling back and forth to her homeland in Manitoba.

"The love and resistance that I have experienced in my Métis community and in the Mi'kmaw communities I have been a part of is the same love and resistance that I hope readers find in my book," Andrea told the *Winnipeg Free Press* in 2024.

"That ability to love is itself a form of resistance."

ROBERT WRIGHT

In the final moments of Deborah Castrilli's short film *Framework*, Robert Wright asks the other two subjects: "What's your queer Black dream?" Robert, Amber Zaza, and Chloé Bramble sit around a dinner table draped in a vintage white-and-gold floral cloth, discussing their queer Black identities.

"I am slowly accepting my status as an elder in my communities," Robert answers when it is his turn. "And part of accepting that role of elder is recognizing—not giving up on your own life by any means, I've got a lot of living left to do, let me tell you—but my responsibility is to pave the road that someone else is going to travel."

Robert has already paved a great many of those roads.

A queer Black man, single father, and deeply spiritual person, Robert is a social worker with decades of experience. He has worked with children and families, victims of and people who use violence (specifically men), people in prison, and within and on behalf of the African Nova Scotian community.

Robert was also the first director of the African Nova Scotian Justice Institute, which strives to achieve justice for Black folks in Nova Scotia navigating legal and government systems.

Robert's contributions were honoured by Halifax Pride in 2018, when he was named the festival's ambassador.

"Serving as the ambassador to Pride is a reminder...that we need to always look to and care for people who are on the fringes," Robert told CBC at the time.

“My dream,” Robert tells Amber and Chloé in *Framework*, “Is to find my proper role as the queer Black elder now, in this space, in this community, so that people like yourselves aren’t having to do that work alone, and that you have a place to rest where you are celebrated and seen and held and cared for in all of your loves and in all of your losses.”

MADONNA DOUCETTE

"My gay agenda is to make Nova Scotia a safer, healthier, and happier place for two-spirit, lesbian, gay, bisexual, and transgender youth," Madonna Doucette told *PNI Atlantic News* in 2022. And as the director for the Cape Breton Youth Project (for 2SLGBTQIA+ youth), Madonna has done just that.

Born in New Waterford, Cape Breton, Madonna is a "proud coal miner's daughter" who became a single mother of three at twenty-five years old. Having discovered that she was a lesbian in her late twenties, Madonna was not public about her sexuality until she was thirty-five.

"I feel the need to be a role model and to be an example of harm reduction in real time," Madonna says in the book *Smashing It, Conversations with Influential Women on Cape Breton Island.* "The cost of a person's mental health for being **closeted** is extremely high."

After telling her three children she was a lesbian, Madonna came out in a big way, launching an online magazine dedicated to queer Cape Breton stories, *Coastal Braid.* It was her way to make a difference for the growing 2SLGBTQIA+ community in her beloved home.

While giving a talk at a series called Powered by Passion, Madonna said the positive reaction from readers made her realize something: "we're sort of hungry in this area to connect as a community even more than we have already done."

Madonna was first hired by the AIDS Coalition of Cape Breton, now the Ally Centre of Cape Breton, to be their LGBT community educator. During her time with the Coalition, she partnered with the (2SLGBTQIA+) Youth

Project (YP), which eventually hired her to staff the organization on the island. She now refers to herself as a "professional queer."

With the Youth Project, Madonna has travelled all over the beautiful isle of Cape Breton, talking to students, educators, businesses, and others about gender and sexual diversity. She has also connected queer and trans youth to life-changing (and often life-saving) supports, provided a twice-weekly hot meal to participants, organized events such as Queer Prom, helped the YP open its own physical space, and much more!

Her proudest accomplishment, though? "I have so many young adults out there who are living amazing lives that are authentic," Madonna says in *Smashing It*. "They're succeeding in school. They have families or jobs. They are now role models for the next generation. I could fill a book with success stories."

JEREMY DUTCHER

"I'm just making music at the intersections at which I find myself," Jeremy Dutcher tells CBC's *In the Making* while sitting in their parents' home.

Jeremy explores the intersection between their two-spirit and Wolastoqiyik identities in their second album, *Motewolonuwok*. Translated from Wolastoqey, it means "people of great spiritual power" and can refer to two-spirit or Indigenous queer people. On their second album, Jeremy is singing to these people, their/nekom's people. (Jeremy also uses the gender-neutral pronoun "nekom.")

"Two-spirit people and gender-diverse people have always been a part of our circles," Jeremy tells the CBC's *Unreserved*. "I've gone around this country, and I've met people that were raised by their grandparents in the language, and they tell stories about the fact that two-spirit people, queer and gender diverse people are just a part of our fabric. And not even just a part, but a very important part, a spiritual part."

Jeremy's debut record, *Wolastoqiyik Lintuwakonawa* (English translation: *The Songs of the People of the Beautiful River*), was carefully composed around old wax cylinder recordings of their Wolastoqiyik ancestors singing traditional songs. Wolastoqey is an endangered language, which Jeremy's own mother was punished for speaking at Canadian **day school**. Jeremy's mother has since created a Wolasotqey immersion school, Kehkimin Wolastoqey.

Accepting the prestigious Polaris Prize for *Wolastoqiyik Lintuwakonawa*, Jeremy declared: "Canada, you are in the midst of an Indigenous renaissance," a renaissance in which Jeremy plays an important part. Jeremy was the first artist to win the Polaris Prize twice, the second time for *Motewolonuwok*.

A "little queer kid" from Fredericton, New Brunswick, a member of Tobique First Nation (Neqotkuk), Jeremy grew up with a love of musical theatre. They blossomed into a classically trained tenor who has carried their music and language to some of the most exciting stages across Turtle Island. From the Junos to famed Canadian folk singer Joni Mitchell's seventy-fifth birthday to *Canada's Drag Race*, Jeremy proudly represents their identities.

Poised in front of a piano on the stage of Massey Hall in Toronto at the end of 2023, his hair in three long braids, Jeremy tells the crowd:

"It feels cool to take this little gay road show, this little rainbow fantastic extravaganza we're doing, out into the little towns too. Representation, it makes a difference. When you get to go and shine light into places that don't have a lot of queer representation, it's a gift to get to do that."

LIANE KHOURY/ ليان خوري

When Liane Khoury decided to start Queer Arabs Halifax in 2015, she put Arabic–language posters advertising the group up and down one of the busiest streets in Halifax: Spring Garden Road. Almost instantly, another queer Arab emailed her, interested.

Liane (pronounced *Lay-an*) was eighteen when she moved to Halifax, Nova Scotia (Kjipuktuk), from Amman, Jordan, for university. With roots in Jerusalem and Haifa, Liane's family was displaced from Palestine by the Israeli **occupation**. She identifies as queer and bisexual.

"Before I started the group, I found myself extremely lonely, and I felt like nobody gets me and what I'm about," Liane told *The Queer Arabs* podcast. "It was weird trying to separate the queer and being Arab..."

When another Arab friend confessed they were questioning their sexuality, Liane decided to make her idea from a few years earlier a reality and start the group. At that first meeting at a coffee shop "everybody looked so happy to be there," Liane told the podcast. "So much so that I was like 'this is what I was meant to do.'"

Queer Arabs Halifax is a safe space and social group where LGBTQIA+ people of Arab and Middle Eastern descent in Halifax can be themselves. The group has organized coffee hangouts, a candlelight vigil, a showcase of Palestinian short films, and an anti-pinkwashing (see the sidebar on page 79) campaign.

Through the group, Liane has found her **chosen family** and community.

Queer Arabs isn't the only 2SLGBTQIA+ space that Liane has helped to create. Liane supported her friend, social worker Patrick Maubert, in the founding of UNtoxicated Queers, a group for queer and trans people who have experienced addiction to drugs or alcohol. Those meetings, which began virtually in 2020, were attended by people across North America (also known as Turtle Island in some Indigenous cultures).

In her day job as a health promoter for the Nova Scotia Health Authority, Liane has focused on both the 2SLGBTQIA+ and newcomer communities, and those who (like her) identify as both.

In *The Queer Arabs* podcast episode, the hosts ask Liane and a fellow group member what they wish the queer community knew about queer and trans folks from the Middle East and North Africa.

Liane's response is simple, but powerful.

"We exist."

PINKWASHING

The term "pinkwashing" can be used to describe a government or corporation that promotes itself as 2SLGBTQIA+ friendly without really supporting the community and/or to cover up its human rights or environmental violations. This can also be called "rainbow-washing."

For example, a company may put out a 2SLGBTQIA+ Pride–themed advertising campaign to sell products but doesn't have any supports for its queer employees. Or a country may promote itself as a tourist or travel destination for 2SLGBTQIA+ people to distract from a history of colonization and racial discrimination.

JAY AARON ROY

When Jay Aaron Roy opened his comic and collectables shop, Cape & Cowl, in Sackville, Nova Scotia, his goal was to build a space that would have helped a young him.

"There's so many youth that need somewhere to go in Sackville, so I just try to provide them with a fun space that's safe," Jay told the CBC. "I'm like the bodyguard there. There's a zero tolerance for bullying here."

Growing up in Fall River, Jay first felt his "trans status" around four years old. He told an audience at an International Women's Day event about being "mistaken for female [at birth] before I had the ability to think critically and self-advocate."

Jay opened Cape & Cowl in 2014, the same year he was voted Halifax's Best Activist by *The Coast.* Readers recognized Jay for his work with the Youth Project and his efforts to get the provincial government to drop the requirement to have surgery before you could change your gender marker on your ID. (For more on gender markers, see the sidebar on page 26.) During Halifax Pride in 2021, Jay was recognized by the Nova Scotia Rainbow Action Project with its Rising Star Award for his advocacy and leadership.

The shop itself is a physical manifestation of Jay's activism, which (much like his heart) he wears on his sleeve.

Cape & Cowl includes a drop-in space for youth, officially named the Leighann Wichman Safe Place for the former executive director of the Youth Project, who passed away the same year Jay opened the shop. Leighann and Jay bonded over their shared love of geek culture when

Jay was working at Halifax comic store Strange Adventures, and she encouraged him to volunteer for the YP. In the Safe Place, youth and families can hang out, play video games, borrow queer and trans books and zines, and attend Dungeons & Dragons, Magic: The Gathering, and Pokémon events, art programs, and more.

Jay also uses his position as a small-business owner to increase visibility for the trans community. In 2017 Jay had *trans-owned business: representation matters* painted on the front of the store, bordered by a trans flag. When trans comic artist Sophie Labelle shared the image on social media, Jay heard from people from as far away as Australia, thanking him for being so visible.

"There's a lot of trans youth who are coming out," Jay said to the CBC about the mural. "They need to see that we're here, we're queer, and we own comic book stores too."

LARA LEWIS

The first time Lara Lewis acted on stage, she was nine years old in a school play. A drama kid in high school, Lara graduated from Dalhousie University with a theatre degree that focused on things like playwriting, play development, and directing.

On her website, Lara describes herself as a "queer mixed Mi'kmaw/settler theatre artist." She is passionate about telling new stories or telling old stories in a new way. "Especially queer work, and ESPECIALLY queer work in Mi'kma'ki and the Maritimes," she says.

It's fitting then that Lara's first professional acting job was the play *Princes Rules* by the Halifax-based queer theatre and events company HEIST. She also played gay on stage in *Fruit Machine,* written by New Brunswicker Alex Rioux. The play illustrates Canada's attempts to rid (purge) the military and government of 2SLGBTQ+ people (see the sidebar on the next page).

Lara has been instrumental in creating space for other theatre makers and artists in Halifax. In 2023 she won Theatre Nova Scotia's Merritt Award for Outstanding Volunteer for her work with the Bus Stop Theatre Co-operative, a performance space owned by artists and, as she told *Blackout Podcast*, her "favourite place in the world . She was later named an interim (temporary) executive director for the space.

She has also had a hand in running Halifax's Mayworks Festival of Working People and the Arts and the Halifax Fringe Festival for new and experimental works of theatre.

If you recognize Lara, it may be from, well, all of that, or it may be from her role as a founding member of the queer- and trans-worker–owned Glitter Bean Café Co-op. (She and her fellow co-operative coffee shop–owning pals are profiled in another book in this series, *Amazing Atlantic Canadian Women*.)

"Ultimately, more than theatre as a thing in and of itself, my primary interest is doing cool things with friends," Lara says. "I think we can work to steward spaces that carry that spirit of community, sorority, and most importantly, play."

CANADA'S 2SLGBTQ+ PURGE

A period, roughly between the 1950s and 1990s, when the Canadian government attempted to find and fire queer people from the military and other federal government jobs. 2SLGBTQIA+ federal employees were harassed, subjected to violence, and many suffered mental health challenges as a result. In 2017, after many years of pressure from purge survivors and supporters, the Canadian government gave a formal apology for the purge. In 2018, after the survivors sued, the federal government agreed to pay purge survivors for their suffering.

SHIANNE GORDON

Shianne Gordon believes that "everyone has the right to heal, not just survive." So much so, that she has devoted her life to helping others do just that.

For Shianne, the drive to do good comes from "knowing first-hand what it's like to live a dangerous and risky life and not knowing how to find safety at a young age," she says. Growing up in Dartmouth, Nova Scotia, Shianne was exposed to "a lot of things that are going on in the streets", including drugs, she said in a Boys and Girls Club video. The Boys and Girls Club (now called BGC) in Dartmouth North gave her the space to be a kid and act silly, something she didn't have elsewhere in her life. That, and some much-needed stability.

Later, working for that very club gave Shianne the opportunity to provide the same experience to other young people in her community. The care she received at the BGC allowed Shianne to "transition my life and grow into who I was always meant to be" as a two-spirit, African Nova Scotian, and Indigenous person. Because of this, Shianne feels a personal responsibility to be there for others who feel unheard or unsafe, to provide that safe space for them. That includes people who have survived sexual violence. As a staff person for the Halifax-based Avalon Sexual Assault Centre and East Preston Family Resource Centre, Shianne works with communities across Nova Scotia to find ways to prevent that violence, and alongside survivors to help them access supports and services.

In 2025 Shianne received the distinction of a Governor General's Award in Commemoration of the Persons Case, which recognizes Canadians who work to end gender-based violence (see the sidebar below) and empower women and girls. That same year, she was chosen to be part of a group that gave the Nova Scotia government advice about gender-based violence.

Through her work, Shianne is able to see people who have gone through something very hard grow and develop healthy habits, boundaries, relationships, hobbies, and more. To learn to love themselves, and others, again.

"I have been blessed to also witness what happens when those safer spaces are provided and we show up with care to those in need of it," she says.

GENDER-BASED VIOLENCE

The United Nations describes "gender-based violence" (GBV) as "harmful acts directed at an individual based on their gender. It is rooted in gender inequality, the abuse of power, and harmful norms." This violence can be verbal (hate speech, slurs) physical (hurting someone), mental (isolating or intimidating someone), or sexual violence (abuse or exploitation).

Women, girls, and gender diverse people are more likely to experience gender-based violence in their lifetime.

The Action Atlantic website includes a list of support networks available in Atlantic Canada to any youth facing GBV: **actionnowatlantic.ca/community-organizations**

CARLY "CJ" JACKSON

It's Pride night at the Sceptres hockey game in Toronto, and goalie Carly "CJ" Jackson is starting in net for their first Professional Women's Hockey League (PWHL) game. Toronto is tied with the New York Sirens 1:1, and it comes down to a shootout in overtime: if CJ blocks this shot, the Sceptres win. They make the save and skate victorious into the arms of their fellow players to celebrate. CJ is named player of the game in what the Toronto Sceptres's Instagram account calls "a fairytale debut" in front of 8,532 people in the stands.

The only openly non-binary player in the PWHL in the 2025 season, CJ is a fan favourite, due in part to that openness about their gender identity and queerness. Born and raised in Amherst, Nova Scotia, CJ first came out as lesbian and queer in their senior year at the University of Maine. They became a hometown hero when their then-team, the Toronto Six, won the league championship and they were the 2025 Parade Marshall for Cumberland Pride in Amherst.

“I feel really gracious to represent what I do for a lot of people,” CJ told the PWHL’s *Jocks in Jills* podcast. “There’s something really powerful in being seen and feeling heard and feeling understood, and I think that I represent that for people.” They express that queerness, in part, by dressing “more masculine” off the ice, including wearing a suit for their pre-game walk in.

Oh, and there’s their infamous mullet (an iconic haircut in the queer and trans community). Fans have worn mullet wigs at games, and a gender-neutral clothing brand sells a CJ-inspired “magic mullet” T-shirt. CJ told CFL.ca that cutting their hair helped them accept their queerness.

“I think hockey has been kind of the conduit of self-love, really, and feeling a lot of power in who I am,” CJ, who made the move to Seattle’s PWHL team in 2025, told *Hockey News*. “There were times in my personal life where I really struggled, but hockey has always been the consistent thing that has brought me back to my sense of self. And it’s probably the place where I feel most like myself at any time in my life.”

CHAPTER V

MAKING ART

“*Art...sometimes has a way of sneaking its way into our hearts and minds and cells in a way that mere information can't.*”

Elizabeth Glenn-Copeland

“*Poetry, writing, sharing—it's a really valuable role to play in society.*”

Tanya Davis

“*Any opportunities to write or create, I take.*”

francesca ekwuyasi

CHARLES HENRY DANIELLE

"On Thursday, May 1, there died at St. John's, Newfoundland, the strangest man in America," reads a newspaper clipping about the passing of Charles Henry Danielle in 1902. While Charles Henry Danielle was surely not the "strangest man", he likely didn't blend in in 1800s Newfoundland. It might have been the castle. Colleen Quigley, head of Memorial University's archives, instead calls Charles "very eccentric, extravagant, fabulous."

Born in 1830 in Baltimore, Maryland, Charles moved to Newfoundland in the 1860s. According to a letter written by a friend, Charles "was a great lover of men." Before taking residence in Newfoundland, Charles made a living as an actor and costume maker in Brooklyn, New York. There, he dressed local men for the balls (dances). "He transformed Brooklynites into courtiers and kings," reads an article in an unknown newspaper, now in Newfoundland and Labrador's Digital Queer Archive.

Sometimes referred to as Professor Danielle, Charles was also a dance instructor. An ad in the *Harbour Grace Standard* newspaper announced "to the fashionable and respectable public of Harbor Grace" that Danielle would hold classes in the "now popular and fashionable Dances" on a Tuesday evening in 1890. Charles's students later held a Grand Fancy Costume Ball in Harbour Grace, Newfoundland.

In 1896 Charles built an eight-sided, four-storey house, crowned Octagon Castle. A flyer for the castle heralds the hotel and summer resort as a "marvel in architecture and adornments, [which] elicits the wonder and admiration of all guests and visitors." Its grand rooms were draped with silk and satin, Chinese lanterns, fans, and other ornamentation. Most famously, Octagon Castle featured Charles's custom-made coffin, wrapped in black satin, trimmed with lace, and adorned with a botanical motif, a cross, and a harp.

Charles left *very specific* hand-written instructions for his wake and funeral, to be carried out by his heir (an employee and friend whom he legally adopted), to whom Charles also left Octagon Castle. Charles's funeral procession was witnessed by thousands of curious Newfoundlanders when he died of heart trouble at age seventy-two. Charles's archives serve as some of the earliest physical evidence of queer life in Atlantic Canada, an important reminder that we have always been here.

WHAT ARE ARCHIVES?

Archives are places where people keep documents from the past that teach us about our history and give us information to help us understand our present. 2SLGBTQIA+ communities have created their own archives to document and protect our unique histories.

In the Atlantic provinces, local 2SLGBTQIA+ archival materials are kept in Newfoundland and Labrador's **Digital Queer Archive** by the NL Queer Research Initiative; Nova Scotia's **LGBT Seniors Archive** at Dalhousie University and the **Queer Heritage Initiative Collection** at the Provincial Archives of New Brunswick. The **Two-Spirit Archives** are housed at the University of Winnipeg Archives; the **ArQuives** in Toronto is a 2SLGBTQIA+ archive that preserves history from across Canada; and the **Transgender Archives** are kept at the University of Victoria Libraries.

ERICA RUTHERFORD

In 1993 Prince Edward Island–based artist and transgender woman Erica Rutherford published her autobiography, *Nine Lives*, with Charlottetown's Ragweed Press. This was decades before memoirs by transgender celebrities were widely published.

Nine Lives refers to the various eras of Erica's life. It spans multiple continents (Europe, Africa, and North America), jobs, marriages, and her gender **transition**. Throughout her life, Erica worked as an actor, set designer, filmmaker, farmer, women's boutique owner, and professor, though she is best known as an illustrator and painter.

"Certainly I can say that I have had more than my share of variety, and that I have lived with great intensity and never been bored," she writes in *Nine Lives*.

Born in 1923 in Edinburgh, Scotland, Erica was assigned male at birth, and it "was a lifetime preoccupation for her, feeling that she was not living the right gender," Erica's daughter, Susana Rutherford, told the CBC in 2024. Erica underwent gender-affirming surgery in 1976 at the age of fifty-three. (See the sidebar on page 31 for more on gender-affirming health care.)

"I only hope that one day there may be a way of avoiding the terrible conflicts that a transsexual experiences," Erica wrote in her book, using a word that was more commonly used for transgender people at the time. "It would help if society continues to clear away the stereotypical images of male and female."

After a family vacation to Canada with their daughter, Erica and her wife, Gail, bought an old farmhouse in Pinette, PEI. "I felt at home there for the first time since I had come to North America," Erica wrote of the island. Erica and Gail's renovated barn was *the* venue for artist retreats and printmaking workshops, leading to the creation of the Printmaker's Council of PEI.

Erica painted well into her eighties, and her final show was held in Charlottetown's Confederation Centre Art Gallery in 2006. She passed away two years later.

In 2024 Erica became the first PEI artist to have her work shown at the renowned international cultural exhibition, the Venice Biennale in Italy. That year and the year after, the Confederation Centre Art Gallery and National Gallery of Canada both showed selections of her art (also called a "retrospective"). Today, a mural of one of Erica's most well-known paintings can be seen on the side of a building in Charlottetown.

As the headline for an article about Erica's National Gallery show proclaims, Erica "might be the most visionary Canadian artist you've never heard of." With the renewed attention being given to her art and life, Erica hopefully won't be considered "unknown" for much longer.

WALTER BORDEN

In 1974, in the "springtime of [his] twenties," Walter Borden sat down to write the story of his life. After writing eight lines of poetry, he came to the "firm conclusion that I really had nothing else to say," Walter writes in the introduction to his play *The Last Epistle of Tightrope Time.*

Walter would spend forty-eight years building on those eight lines, eventually crafting them into a one-man, semi-autobiographical (meaning, based on his life) play he still performs to this day. "You only get from where you are to where you need to go by inching on your tightrope," Walter writes. The tightrope, you see, is life. Or, as Walter calls it, "some itty bitty madness/between your twilight and your dawn."

"In order to do this work, I would have to live it before I wrote it," he said of the play at the book launch in 2024. "It would be completed in its own time."

The play was one of the first in the country to reflect the experience of being a Black gay man. But Walter didn't set out for that to be so. "Here is a person who happened to be gay [Walter] who wrote about life, which included gay people," he says.

Born in New Glasgow, Nova Scotia, Walter has lived the life of an artist—a playwright, an actor, an author—and also an activist. Most times, those things were intertwined.

In 1965 Walter took up with the African Nova Scotian **civil rights** group the Nova Scotia Project, with cousin Burnley Allan "Rocky" Jones and dear friend Joan Jones. Two years later he was a founding member of the Inglewood Community Players, Nova Scotia's first Black theatre company. In 1967 Walter began his studies in theatre in New York and marched against the Vietnam War.

In 1972 he joined Halifax's (Kjipuktuk's) Neptune Theatre Company, and continued to work for the Black United Front until 1979.

Walter is a commanding and animated stage presence with a voice that CBC has called "liquid gold." The plays that he has chosen over his fifty-plus-year career tackle issues such as race and oppression, and the fight for civil rights.

These plays include *The Adventures of a Black Girl in Search of God, Harlem Duet,* and *Lilies,* in which Walter plays a character that reflects his Black and Indigenous ancestry. No stranger to Shakespeare, Walter has also performed several of the Bard's plays in Ontario's famous Stratford Festival.

"Over the years the activist side of me has determined to no small degree precisely what I would do in theatre," Walter told *Intermission Magazine.* "I always wanted to know that what I was doing on stage, how I was presenting myself on stage, was in some way advancing some aspect of my activism."

MAXIM MAZUMDAR

Maxim Mazumdar's most well-known play is called *Oscar Remembered*. It imagines the love affair between famous Irish poet and playwright Oscar Wilde and Lord Alfred Douglas, an affair which led to Oscar being sent to jail in the late 1890s.

"In the 1970s, homosexuality was still **stigmatized**, and Wilde's name carried an aura of scandal and disrepute," Rhea Rollmann writes in her book, *A Queer History of Newfoundland*. *Oscar Remembered*, she says, was "one of the early creative works that presented Wilde in a different light," showing him in a "positive and heroic way." Today, Oscar Wilde is considered a gay icon, due in part to the efforts of artists such as Maxim.

The one-man play, which Maxim himself performed, toured the United States and Canada, including Ontario's prestigious Stratford Festival.

Maxim was inspired to write *Oscar Remembered* because, as he writes in the foreword for the play, he was "always a little bewitched by Wilde's influence." The play, he continued, "was most inviting because of the risk involved. What depth lay beneath the jewelled words, the conflicting biographies, the chameleon-like letters—this haunted me."

Born in Mumbai, India, in 1952, Maxim was the lead in several professional theatrical productions by the young age of thirteen. Maxim and his mother immigrated to Canada in 1969 after his father's death, and Maxim attended Concordia University in Montreal. While there, he co-founded his first theatre company, opening a small theatre on the outskirts of Montreal after he graduated in 1972.

It was in Stephenville, a town on the west coast of Newfoundland and Labrador, when he was a judge for the 1976 Provincial Drama Festival, that Maxim dreamt up the Stephenville Theatre Festival. Born out of the Provincial Drama Academy (also founded by Maxim), the festival opened three years later.

The Stephenville Theatre Festival attracted audiences from throughout Atlantic Canada, Ontario, and the eastern United States and toured to St. John's and Halifax in the mid- to late 1980s. Today, the festival is the longest-running professional theatre company in Newfoundland and Labrador.

Maxim passed away from the lung condition pulmonary fibrosis in 1988, though it was widely reported that he died of complications due to AIDS.

"The province's arts and culture field owes an outsized debt of gratitude to Maxim Mazumdar, a passionate actor, director, and playwright who for the space of about a decade brought the province's theatre to a global stage," Rhea Rollmann writes in *A Queer History of Newfoundland*.

BEVERLY GLENN-COPELAND AND ELIZABETH GLENN-COPELAND

Beverly Glenn-Copeland ("Glenn") and Elizabeth Glenn-Copeland waltz as they harmonize the lyrics to Glenn's song "Let Us Dance" in their living room.

"The wind blows over hillside, the day greets the dawn, the sun dances down beside this road we are on," they sing. "Let us dance down the road…down the road."

This beautiful scene between husband and wife, and artistic collaborators, closes out a video where they announce Glenn's diagnosis with major cognitive disorder called LATE, which falls under the umbrella of dementia.

"Dementia," according to the Alzheimer Society of Canada, "describes a set of symptoms that may include memory loss, changes in mood, and difficulties with thinking, problem solving, and language."

Though they had planned to stop touring after Glenn's diagnosis, the couple just could not stay home doing word puzzles, Elizabeth explained on the CBC Radio show *Q*. One day Glenn looked at her and said, "maybe this is supposed to extend my life, but I just don't feel like we're living. I have places to go, I have people to see, I have things I want to say still." He credits his ability to continue to tour to "the brilliance of [Elizabeth's] creative vision, which has often gone unnoticed."

"Let Us Dance" is on Glenn's groundbreaking self-released 1986 album *Keyboard Fantasies*, re-released in 2017 to great excitement and acclaim. In 2020 it won the Polaris Heritage Prize, celebrating classic Canadian albums.

It was Leslie Feinberg's novel *Stone Butch Blues* (an early representation of butch and **transmasculine** people) that made Glenn realize he was a trans man.

"I just kind of sat up and went, 'I am transgender.' And I had never put those words to it," Glenn told the CBC. "My whole being just relaxed on a level that it had never relaxed."

In his late fifties, Glenn came out publicly as trans.

Glenn's 2023 album, *The Ones Ahead* (which refers to younger generations), is a meditation on climate change. Much of Elizabeth's work, which includes poetry, theatre, music, and writing workshops, also combines her art with her activism. It explores "eco-despair" (depression about the climate disaster) and creating active hope in its midst. In 2019 she published a book of poetry exploring this, called *Daring to Hope at the Cliff's Edge*.

"Art…sometimes has a way of sneaking its way into our hearts and minds and cells in a way that mere information can't," Elizabeth says in an interview with the *Nurtured by Nature* podcast.

And so, Glenn and Elizabeth make art. In February of 2026 they released the album *Laughter in Summer*, they continued to tour, make theatre, and write a book. Through it all, love has been their "guiding force," as Elizabeth put it to *Nurtured by Nature*.

As Glenn writes in his song "Harbour: Song for Elizabeth": "You're my harbour, my rainbow, my promise of tomorrow."

EVELYN C. WHITE

Journalist and author Evelyn C. White began writing in grade 5.

While living in Seattle, Washington, in the late 1970s, Evelyn took it upon herself to collect books from the local used-bookstore and send reviews to alternative newspapers such as the *Seattle Gay News*. One of her first published reviews was of *The Coming Out Stories*, an early collection of gay and lesbian writing.

Evelyn has always been an openly lesbian writer. The decision to be "out" about her sexuality was greatly influenced by Black writers that came before her, such as James Baldwin and Lorraine Hansberry. "They were never able to speak openly about their sexuality, and in my view, the silence cost them both a great deal," Evelyn says. "I honour them by being free, and freedom is a mighty fine thing."

Born in Chicago, Illinois, Evelyn was raised in Gary, Indiana. Her parents had migrated from the southern United States due to the violence against Black people and because of better opportunities for work. She grew up during a time when the civil rights movement was winning victories for Black people in the US.

After attending graduate school for journalism in New York City and doing an internship at *The Wall Street Journal*, Evelyn got her first reporting job for *The San Francisco Chronicle*, the largest paper in the area.

Evelyn moved to Nova Scotia with her Canadian partner, Joanne, in 2012.

Having interviewed the likes of Oprah Winfrey, Queen Latifah, and Whoopi Goldberg, one of Evelyn's personal career highlights was speaking to civil rights activist icon Rosa Parks. A photograph of the two is one of Evelyn's greatest treasures.

"I am a direct descendant of enslaved Africans who were forbidden, on the penalty of death, to learn how to read or write," Evelyn told the Creative Nova Scotia Leadership Council. "As such, I approach my work as a journalist with uncompromising truth and integrity."

In 1985 Evelyn authored her first book, about Black women in abusive relationships. Later, she spent ten years writing the official biography of *The Color Purple* author, Alice Walker, which was published in 2004. Alice herself told the *King's Journalism Review* that working with Evelyn on *Alice Walker: A Life* "was one of the best and brightest experiences."

Evelyn, said Alice, is a "truth-teller to her soul."

ANN-MARIE MACDONALD

Ann-Marie MacDonald has been writing queer characters, lives, and loves in her widely acclaimed plays and books since the 1980s. Even when producers (people who put on plays) were initially unsure that audiences would accept queer content.

"I feel lucky because I am among the early queer writers who found a wide audience. I earned the trust of my audience early on, in part because I was never closeted," Ann-Marie says. "I know that it took a lot of courage for my younger self to do that, but I also know that at the time I really didn't consider it would be possible to do it any other way."

When *Goodnight Desdemona (Good Morning Juliet)*—a play that featured an onstage kiss between two women—premiered in 1988, it felt "bold, joyous and fun." That bold play won Ann-Marie several awards, and would continue to find audiences throughout the years.

Ann-Marie was born on a Royal Canadian Air Force station in West Germany in 1958 to Cape Bretoners: a Lebanese mother and a father of Scottish origin. As a young girl, she hid her sexuality from her religious parents. When she came out as a lesbian at age twenty-four in the 1980s, her parents confirmed her childhood instincts that she was the "wrong kind of girl," she told the CBC.

Ann-Marie found both comfort and a creative outlet in playing make-believe and drawing cartoons and comic strips and discovered acting by the age of ten.

Her first novel, *Fall on Your Knees*, came out in 1996 to awe, awards, and inclusion in Oprah Winfrey's book club. Ann-Marie is known for writing queer and gender-diverse characters across the ages—from the late 1800s, the 1920s, the mid-1900s, and beyond—because, well, we have existed in all of those times. *Fayne* (2022), which she calls her queerest book yet, centres on an intersex child, one born with a body that doctors couldn't categorize as boy or girl. "A normal human variation that has been **pathologized** to this day," Ann-Marie told *Chatelaine* magazine.

Ann-Marie worked as a consultant when her wife (and frequent creative partner), Alisa Palmer, co-adapted and directed *Fall on Your Knees* as a play, which ran at Halifax's Neptune Theatre, and in three other cities, in 2023. The couple has two grown children.

"I came of age in a world that thought it was absurd of same-sex people to marry one another," MacDonald told the CBC for their *Super Queeros!* series.

"It was like that until I was forty. So getting married and having children is the most surprising thing that has happened to me."

TANYA DAVIS

Growing up in Summerside, Prince Edward Island, Tanya Davis didn't know that people could make a career out of being a writer, and definitely not as a poet. As an adult, her musical poetry (poetry songs, or "pongs" as she has called them) has propelled Tanya as far as Japan and Australia.

In 2024 Tanya was selected to be part of Canada's cultural programming at Expo 2025 in Osaka, Japan, somewhere she had always wanted to visit.

"I'm grateful that my career as an artist is also a vehicle that takes me places," Tanya writes in her Substack newsletter. "It's one of the best parts of the job. I like it now more than ever, now that I feel at home again, back on this little island by the sea."

"It's great to leave," she continues, "but only because I'm always so happy to come back."

As poet laureate for both Halifax and the province of PEI, Tanya worked to promote poetry to as many people as possible. Specifically, "the lessons that need teaching, the ailments that need fixing, and the fires that need putting out," as she wrote for the CBC.

Tanya has found creative ways to popularize poetry throughout her career. Most famously in the viral video *How to Be Alone*, which she created with Andrea Dorfman, and which has millions of views. "If you are at first lonely, be patient," the poem begins before listing all the ways to enjoy one's own company. The poem, now also a book, inspired a Covid-19 pandemic–era sequel, *How to Be at Home*, about how to cope with quarantine. She has also released several spoken-word–infused albums of music, which one music critic compared to lullabies for grown-ups.

Tanya Davis has always wanted to be a writer. Now she's "excited to encourage the next generation of poets and writers and let them know that this is a career option," she said upon being named PEI's poet laureate. For Tanya, who didn't figure out she was queer until after high school, this has included working with the PEI Queer Youth Group Writing Club, helping young writers craft pieces for their book *Are We Friends Now?* The book was published by PEI's Acorn Press in 2023.

"Poetry, writing, sharing—it's a really valuable role to play in society."

FRANCESCA EKWUYASI

Francesca ekwuyasi began writing her first novel, *Butter Honey Pig Bread*, while she was home in Lagos, Nigeria, in 2013. For francesca, the book was a "manifestation of years and years of experimenting and reading but also my lifetime up until now of dreaming," she told *The Walrus* magazine in 2021. The stunning debut is about the relationships amongst a Nigerian mother, who believes that she cursed her family by cheating death, and her twin daughters.

From a lineage of Yoruba and Igbo artists and musicians, francesca first started writing fictional stories in her journal as a child. She dreamt about publishing her own book. "It's a real book that exists for people to read, but it's also a symbol of possibility and a concrete physical reminder that I can do the things I want to do and achieve the goals that like little baby francesca had," she told *The Walrus* magazine.

Born and raised in Lagos, francesca moved to upstate New York for her undergraduate studies and then to Halifax for her graduate degree. In all, *Butter Honey Pig Bread* took seven years to craft. francesca drafted much of it in her head walking around Lagos, Halifax, and Montreal: three of the main places featured in the story.

The novel made quite the impact when published in 2020. It was nominated for several awards, and won the Dayne Ogilvie Prize for LGBTQ2S+ Emerging Writers from the Writers' Trust of Canada. In 2021 it competed against four other books in CBC Radio's annual national literary competition, Canada Reads, placing second. The book has been translated into Italian and German and was published in Nigeria in 2022.

The enthusiastic response to *Butter Honey Pig Bread* encouraged francesca to create more. Expressing herself in a variety of ways, her fiction, non-fiction, and visual art explore themes of family, faith, home, Blackness, and queerness. Her short documentary *Black + Belonging* premiered as part of the Being Black in Halifax collection on CBC Gem, and her videos, prints, and paper cut-outs have been featured in several art galleries.

"Any opportunities to write or create," francesca said during an interview for Nigeria's Ake Arts and Book Festival in 2021, "I take."

JOCE REYOME

"My name is Joce. I'm going to play some songs for ya," Joce Reyome says from the stage of the Orpheum Theatre in Memphis, Tennessee. With their powerful, raspy voice and driving guitar, Joce launched into the performance that would win the 2025 solo/duo category at the world's largest gathering of blues musicians: the International Blues Challenge Finals.

"It feels like a surreal experience," the non-binary singer-songwriter told *Wayves Magazine* of their win. It was their first time in Memphis, and they'd been one of 115 artists competing for the title.

Of Irish, African, Cape Verdean, and Hawaiian descent, Joce was adopted into a white family in the state of Massachusetts. Joce's parents brought them up on the music of the 1960s and 1970s, and they list the likes of Aretha Franklin, Janis Joplin, Otis Redding, and Etta James as inspirations. And, of course, 1980s and 1990s icon Tracy Chapman.

It was in grade 4 that Joce first sang in front of an audience (their classmates) and around middle school when they first picked up a guitar.

Joce moved to Charlottetown, PEI, in 2016 to pursue music at Holland College. Having originally planned to move back to Boston after graduation, Joce ended up booking enough music gigs to stay on the island.

Describing their music as a "bit bluesy, a bit rock, a bit folk", in a Music PEI video, Joce encourages new artists not to let "anybody tell you what you should be doing and what you can't do."

That approach has paid off.

Having played all over the island, by themselves and with a band, Joce's music has earned them accolades from Music PEI. In 2022 Joce won Music PEI's Entertainer of the Year and in 2025 the R&B/Soul Recording of the Year. Nationally, Joce's song "Mr. Rain" was named one of CBC Music's top 100 Canadian songs in 2024.

They've also performed with the PEI Symphony Orchestra, as well as during the East Coast Music Awards, and as part of JUNOfest in Halifax in 2024. In 2025 they travelled to Japan and South Korea for a blues festival.

For Joce, the blues and their identity will be "forever intertwined" they told *Wayves Magazine*.

"Singing the blues is about sharing your stories and your feelings—those for me are always experienced through the lens of queerness."

"I won't ever not be queer, and I won't ever not sing."

HAYDEN LITTLE

By the time she was nineteen, Hayden Little's fiction and poetry had been published in two books.

First, in *Are We Friends Now: An Anthology By and About 2SLGBTQ+ Youth from PEI*, and then alongside other PEI poets in a collection of poems simply entitled, *Home*.

"The goal of being published as early as possible was one I'd quietly set for myself since childhood when I first realized I wanted to be a writer like my mom instead of an artist like my dad," Hayden says.

It was her participation in the Queer Youth Writing Club, created by the PEI Writers' Guild and P.E.E.R.S. Alliance, that first made Hayden a published author in 2023. The space also led Hayden to her queer community, friends, and role models. It was a welcome change from the difficulties she'd experienced as a lesbian and someone living with epilepsy (a brain condition that can cause seizures or loss of consciousness).

That feeling of "otherness" permeates Hayden's fantastical fiction, which features faeries and other mystical, magical creatures. This sense of wonder was nurtured by animated films such as the Irish Selkie story *Song of the Sea* and Japanese classics like *My Neighbor Totoro.*

"I was always so taken in by the curious, untouchable, and always fluctuating world that is that of the supernatural," Hayden says. She wanted to "be the mother of a story" that made readers feel like she did watching those movies with her dad.

Hayden's poem featured in *Home* looks at the theme of home from the perspective of a young person living with the impacts of divorced parents.

Like a lot of Hayden's poetry, it is written from a deeply emotional place in the hope of connecting with others.

By the summer of 2025 Hayden had also finished the first draft of her debut novel. Set in Victorian times (the mid-1800s to early 1900s), the book includes a bisexual main character and a smattering of other queer characters. "...There's always been queer people in the world," Hayden says of the manuscript, "and it's good to remind people of that."

Hayden's goal is to have the work published and to someday be a full-time author.

"I'm willing to work hard and wait for it," she says.

CHAPTER VI

EDUCATION

“*When things aren’t talked about in schools, you think they don’t exist.*”

Meredith J. Batt

“*This is a human rights issue. Kids are entitled to a safe learning environment.*”

Sue Rose

“*I want to be there for the generation to come. They need to see people representative and visible, so they know they are not alone.*”

Veronica Merryfield

HAROLD "HAL" HINDS

"Learn them. Love them. Protect them!"

This is what botanist Harold "Hal" Hinds wrote in the New Brunswick Nature Trust's copy of his influential book *Flora of New Brunswick*, about the province's native plants. These words also beautifully describe Hal's devotion to the lesbian, gay, and bisexual community in New Brunswick and beyond.

Hal took over New Brunswick's first gay liberation organization, Gay Friends of Fredericton (GFF), founded in 1974 by Keith Sly. In 1979 Hal, Allison Brewer (see her profile on page 30), and about twelve other people founded Fredericton Lesbians and Gays (FLAG) in his apartment.

President of FLAG for the first few years, Hal co-organized the fourth Atlantic Gay and Lesbian Conference in Fredericton in 1982 and made speeches at a number of other gay conferences.

According to "A Brief Queer History of New Brunswick" included in the book *Len & Cub: A Queer History* (see the profile on page 126 for more on this amazing book), Hal was also involved in forming several other New Brunswick LGB groups, including AIDS New Brunswick and the New Brunswick Coalition for Human Rights Reform, which pushed the provincial government to include sexual orientation in its human rights law. Doing so would protect 2SLGBQ people from being discriminated against due to their sexual orientation when it came to things such as employment and housing. (This finally happened in 1992!)

"Often I'm involved in getting things started, but after a while I drop out because I'm not interested in…the nitty-gritty of keeping things going,"

Hal told Tom Warner in an interview for Tom's book *Never Going Back: A History of Queer Activism in Canada*. "But I like to make sure things happen."

Hal died in 2001 from complications due to HIV/AIDS. He was in his early sixties.

In 2008 the Government of New Brunswick named a forest near Woodstock the Hal Hinds Forest to recognize Hal's significant contributions to botany in the province. It is one of the most biologically diverse hardwood forests in Atlantic Canada. There is also a Hal Hinds hiking trail in Odell Park, Fredericton.

SUSAN "SUE" ROSE

In 2009, Susan ("Sue") Rose made her way up the west coast of Newfoundland, conducting a workshop called "Making Queerness Visible" in fifteen high schools from Plum Point to Codroy Valley. In all, she reached over twelve hundred students.

Sometimes, when Sue arrived at a school, staff would say: "Welcome, but we don't have any queer students in this community," she said in Egale's guide to LGBTQ Role Models and Symbols. Sue knew that wasn't the case. It was more likely that students didn't feel comfortable or safe sharing their sexual orientation or gender identity.

Sue did the tour as a representative for Canada's national 2SLGBTQIA+ advocacy organization, Egale. Before joining Egale, she had been a teacher for over twenty years.

"Because of some stressful experiences and watching students needing a positive role model, I needed to come out and did so very publicly," Sue told the *Memorial University Gazette*.

In 1997 Newfoundland and Labrador changed its human rights code to protect people from being fired from their jobs because they were lesbian, gay, bisexual, or queer. The next year, the CBC interviewed Sue at home with her partner. "I knew my life would change forever," Sue said. And it did.

Sue retired early from teaching due to homophobia she faced from students and parents. Some parents even removed their children from her class due to her sexuality. Joining Egale was another way for her to work with, educate, support, and protect young people.

"This is a human rights issue," says Rose. "Kids are entitled to a safe learning environment."

Sue's activism started in the early 1990s, when she helped start the lesbian activist group Newfoundland Amazon Network, or NAN, in 1994. Her home was the site of many a meeting, as well as a lesbian phone line women called for support and information. NAN organized dances and other social events and fought for the provincial government to change the human rights act to protect lesbian, gay, bisexual, and queer people from discrimination.

Celebrated for her commitment to 2SLGBTQIA+ activism and students, Sue received the 2017 Newfoundland and Labrador Human Rights Commission's Human Rights Award, and in 2020, the Order of Newfoundland and Labrador (ONL). When receiving the ONL, Sue was written about as follows: "Ms. Rose risked her career by becoming a voice to challenge the status quo and began a lifelong journey of education and training in the hope of building a more inclusive province."

VERONICA MERRYFIELD

"I look forward to a day when we no longer have to talk about the need for acceptance as it becomes the norm and uncomment-worthy," Veronica Merryfield writes in the 2021 article "I am transgender, I am intersex, I am me," adding, "I hold hope that this will happen in my lifetime."

As an outspoken transgender, intersex, pansexual woman, educator, and community organizer, Veronica has done much to make that a reality.

Born and raised in England, Veronica knew at four years old that she was not a boy. Unfortunately, when she told her parents, they were not supportive. There was no one to tell her what being transgender was and that it was okay to be trans. As a young adult, Veronica was subjected to "conversion therapy," a damaging and unscientific practice meant to "cure" people of being queer or trans and turn them straight and **cisgender**.

"I thought I was the only one and there was something really wrong with me," Veronica said during an online panel organized by the Impact Organizations of Nova Scotia (IONS). In the video, Veronica wears a Pride flag dress, against the background of an intersex flag flanked by two more Pride flags.

Finally, at age twenty-three, Veronica was able to get help to start living as herself. With a background in electronic and computer engineering, her paid work now focuses on Diversity, Equity, and Inclusion (DEI) education (see sidebar below) with governments, universities, schools, non-profits, and businesses.

"People don't necessarily understand a trans history unless they've lived it," Veronica told TELILE 24/7 community TV. "So me talking about that and talking about some of the difficulties that I've had growing up is part of this education piece so people understand."

Since moving to Cape Breton in 2016, Veronica has volunteered with various women's groups (she was the first transgender woman to chair Sydney's women's centre!) and sexual health organizations, Pride Cape Breton, as well as the advisory council for the Marion Bridge Elementary school.

DIVERSITY, EQUITY, AND INCLUSION

"Diversity, Equity, and Inclusion" (DEI) refers to education and conversation about cultures, identities, and experiences that are less often represented in society, and sometimes even excluded from society, with the goal of making spaces, institutions, laws, etc. more fair and just.

In 2021 Veronica founded the Cape Breton Transgender Network to increase transgender visibility in Cape Breton and as a source for education and support. In 2023 she received a Nova Scotia Human Rights Award "in recognition of her dedication to advancing equity and advocating for the rights of members of the 2SLGBTQIA+ community." Recently, she became the first transgender woman to sit on Nova Scotia's Status of Women Advisory Council.

"I want to be visible for those who, for whatever reason, can't be out," she says in a *PNI Atlantic News* article about Pride Cape Breton. "I want to be there for the generation to come. They need to see people representative and visible, so they know they are not alone."

DR. MARGARET ROBINSON

"I identify as bisexual, queer, and two-spirit, and sort of in that order," Dr. Margaret Robinson tells Jessica Webber in a Dartmouth Heritage Museum interview. "I came out as bisexual, then later as queer, and then eventually as two-spirit. And now I just use them all."

Margaret got an inkling that she may be attracted to women while living in an all-girls residence at Saint Mary's University. When she saw a flyer from the Youth Project asking something like *do you think you might be gay, lesbian, or bisexual?* that last word "explained everything."

"The puzzle for me had always been: Well, I know I'm attracted to men, but I'm also attracted to women, so that's not really a lesbian," she says in the interview. "So as soon as I saw the word ["bisexual"] I was like 'that's the thing, that's me.'"

Margaret, who is of Scottish, Irish, and Mi'kmaw ancestry (she is a member of Lennox Island First Nation), wrote for the column "Bi Lines" in

Sirens magazine in 2002: "My experience as a bi-racial woman informs the way I look at bisexuality. Just as I can't identify which parts of my body or psyche are Scottish and which are [Mi'kmaw], I can't compartmentalize my sexuality into lesbian and straight."

Biphobia, and a lack of representation within the queer community, encouraged Margaret to do whatever she could to increase public awareness of bisexuality and create bisexual community. She got involved in the early days of Halifax Pride, and over twenty years in Toronto, was involved in various bisexual groups and helped organize the ninth annual International Conference on Bisexuality (BiCon).

"Bisexual space, the few times I've experienced that, that was amazing," Margaret says in the Dartmouth Heritage Museum interview. "You didn't have to explain everything, the people in the room understand right away."

Dr. Robinson's passion for her Mi'kmaw, bisexual, and two-spirit identities has also been a big part of her academic career. At Dalhousie University in Halifax (Kjipuktuk), she is appointed in the departments of English and of Sociology and Social Anthropology; served as Canada Research Chair in Reconciliation, Gender & Identity; and created the Mi'kmaw Cultural Research Lab. She has researched and written about bisexual women's mental health, poverty within the 2SLGBTQIA+ community, and the similarities and differences between bisexual and two-spirit identities.

TWO-SPIRIT IDENTITY

Of her own two-spirit identity, Margaret says: "I see two-spirit as primarily about gender and primarily about my role in regard to my Indigenous community.... So to me, I think that connection to embodying masculinity and femininity is an important part of it."

From *One Harbour, 2SLGBTQIA+ Stories of Halifax and Dartmouth*, an interview with Dartmouth Heritage Museum

RHEA ROLLMANN

As an award-winning journalist, Rhea Rollmann would often come across bits and pieces of Newfoundland's queer and trans history and dream about putting it all together, somewhere.

In 2023 she did just that and published *A Queer History of Newfoundland*, the first book about the island's 2SLGBTQIA+ history.

"It's hard to describe just how powerful it was," Rhea told the CBC about researching and writing the book. She knew there had always been queer people in Newfoundland and Labrador, but didn't know just how deep the history was.

The book is the result of an astounding 150 interviews with queer and trans Newfoundlanders and many deep dives into the local archives, media, and court records. Its pages hold so many stories—from the lesbian life partners who helped working people fight for their rights in 1930s rural Newfoundland to trans people who grew up in coastal outports in the 1950s and 1960s to the province's first formal gay and lesbian group in the early 1970s, and beyond. (The book focuses on Newfoundland, the island, as opposed to Newfoundland and Labrador, the province. Labrador has its own rich history that Rhea believed deserves a more detailed telling than she would be able to give it at that time, as a non-Labradorian.)

The reaction to the book has been overwhelmingly positive. It has had to be reprinted several times to keep up with sales!

"I certainly feel proud, but I feel especially proud of the community," Rhea told the CBC. The people who deserve praise, she added, are the early activists, some of whom lost jobs, family, and friends. "You know, their courage was what needs to be celebrated."

Rhea remembers questioning her own gender identity at age ten during a classroom conversation about what students wanted to be when they grew up. When Rhea looked into her own future, she could only envision growing into a woman, not a man.

Transphobia, including from her grade 6 teacher, as well as a lack of information, supports, and health care, delayed Rhea's transition until later in life. An article about trans people transitioning later in life encouraged Rhea to come out as a proud queer lesbian trans woman just before the Covid-19 pandemic took hold.

Today Rhea uses queer and trans joy (see the sidebar on page 123) to fight back against anti-2SLGBTQIA+ hate.

"I hope that is the overarching sentiment that emerges from the book—the beauty of these lives lived and the love that propelled activists in their fight to build a better world," she told *Atlantic Books Today* magazine. "That remains the source of queer strength and power."

QUEER AND TRANS JOY

The feeling of joy that 2SLGBTQIA+ people can get from feeling free and safe to be themselves; seeing their identity(ies) reflected in wider society and/or media; having their queerness and/or transness accepted and celebrated in various ways; being surrounded by other queer and trans people; finding and expressing the beauty in their queer and/or trans identity, and much, much more.

Examples can include: meeting and sharing space with other queer and/or trans people; wearing clothes, makeup, and/or jewellery that affirm your gender or sexual identity; watching a TV show or movie with positive representation of 2SLGBTQIA+ characters; attending a Pride or other event that celebrates the diversity of the 2SLGBTQIA+ community; or experiencing either romantic or platonic (friendly) queer/trans love.

DR. MAX LIBOIRON

Dr. Max Liboiron is a scientist and plastic pollution researcher who likes to work on so-called *impossible problems*. "It means I can find what makes it impossible and change it," they say in a YouTube video for the Marine Environmental Observation, Prediction and Response Network (MEOPAR).

Max is the director for Memorial University's Civic Laboratory for Environmental Action Research (CLEAR) lab, headquartered in St. John's, Newfoundland and Labrador. In the documentary *GUTS*, Max describes what they do as poking around water and in food webs (an ecosystem's interconnected food chains, showing what eats what), looking for very small plastics. They then report what types and amounts of plastics they find and what Newfoundlanders and Labradorians should and shouldn't be concerned about.

CLEAR is a science lab that does things differently. Max is of Red River Métis (see the sidebar on page 70) and settler descent, and they, and CLEAR, do their research with an **anti-colonial** and feminist approach.

"We want to change the future of science," Max says in the MEOPAR video. "How science is done and by who."

To be "anti-colonial" in this situation means to not take advantage of the land, wildlife, and Indigenous population for science's sake. CLEAR only conducts research where it has been invited by the Indigenous community. All of the lab's research questions come from that community, and their findings are brought back to community for review and input. It also means that CLEAR gives their samples—fish guts!—back to the ecosystem they came from and doesn't use toxic chemicals.

Researchers for CLEAR include young people, trans and gender-diverse people, people without a formal education in science, and Elders.

According to Max, 80-85% of the garbage on Newfoundland and Labrador's shorelines is plastic. Most is single-use packaging, fishing gear, and cigarette butts.

The solution, they say, is to slow down how much plastic we produce. Even though it is one of the longest-lasting human-made materials available, there was a time in our not-so-distant past when we didn't rely on plastic for our packaging.

Along with having a university education in visual arts, Max has authored or co-authored two books, including *Pollution Is Colonialism*. Max uses their arts background to creatively solve problems in the CLEAR lab and knows that humans can use our creativity to find more sustainable alternatives to plastic too!

"We have some skills, and we have some knowledge to deal with very long-term and very grave problems—and still flourish, and laugh, as part of our living," they told the *Watershed Sentinel*.

DUSTY GREEN AND MEREDITH J. BATT

Dusty Green was an intern in the Provincial Archives of New Brunswick when they first saw the photos. The rare images were of two young men in rural New Brunswick in the early 1900s, Len and Cub, and they were shown displaying a clear affection for each other, long before same-sex attraction was socially acceptable.

These were the earliest known images of a same-sex romantic relationship in the Maritimes. For Dusty, they confirmed the existence of long-ago queer history. The two men were described as "boyfriends" by the person who donated the pictures. "Len and Cub broke things open for me and got me really excited about queer history," Dusty told the New Brunswick College of Craft and Design. Dusty was made aware of the Len and Cub photos after stumbling upon another collection of photographs in the archives, of First World War prisoners of war in drag.

In 2015 Dusty founded the Queer Heritage Initiative of New Brunswick (QHINB). He was joined by archivist Meredith J. Batt in 2019, who assisted in setting up the original collection of 2SLGBTQIA+ materials in the provincial archives. Growing up in New Brunswick, neither Dusty nor Meredith learned about queer history in the classroom or saw themselves represented in New Brunswick's past. "When things aren't talked about in schools, you think they don't exist," Meredith said during a 2021 panel. In addition to its educational events, the QHINB developed lesson plans to promote New Brunswick's queer past.

Through the years, the photographs of Len and Cub, known affectionately as "the boys," stuck with Dusty and Meredith. So much of the story was remarkable: that these two men loved each other when it could be dangerous to do so, that Len had the means (a car and family cabins) to keep their relationship private and the technology (a self-timed camera) to document it; and that those photographs were not destroyed.

It is sadly unsurprising for the time period that Len was eventually driven out of his hometown in the 1930s for being a homosexual.

Dusty and Meredith have worked together to tell Len and Cub's story through gallery exhibits and a book titled *Len & Cub: A Queer History*. The book has also been optioned by Elliot Page's production company with the hopes of creating a future TV series based on Len and Cub's story. They were recognized for it all with a Platinum Jubilee Medal in 2022, an honour meant to recognize Canadians who "have been exemplary in their service to others."

"Making these records was sort of like an act of defiance," Meredith said in an interview with the CBC regarding Len and Cub's pictures.

An act of defiance that has echoed, thanks in large part, to the efforts of Dusty Green and Meredith J. Batt.

EVELYN BRADLEY

In 2020 Evelyn Bradley moved from South Carolina, USA, to Charlottetown, PEI, with her wife to start a Diversity, Equity, and Inclusion (DEI) business (see the sidebar on page 117).

"Yes, I'm a Black lesbian from the southern US states who has chosen to make a life in Canada's smallest province," Evelyn Bradley wrote in a CBC opinion piece.

Raised in the suburbs of Atlanta, Georgia, Evelyn cheekily refers to herself as a "Gay from Away." (The term riffs on the term "Come from Away," referring to someone who moved from outside of the Atlantic provinces.) In 2025 Evelyn was granted Canadian citizenship.

As a DEI consultant, Evelyn spends her days "simplifying complex concepts and problems so that people understand how they apply them to their own lives," she says. "DEI has to be something that people feel they can do. It has to be organic and natural, and my job is to remind people that they do have the skills to tackle equity, cultural humility, and bias."

Evelyn's approach is very "hey, you can do this. Just because it's new doesn't mean you aren't equipped," she says.

As a former grade 8 English teacher, Evelyn's passion for education shines through in all she does. Whether it's a podcast with episodes on the undertold history of Black PEI, her opinion column on CBC Radio, or former TV cooking show, *Worth Our Salt*, Evelyn's focus is learning, dialogue, and teaching.

Another prominent theme in Evelyn's work is her love for PEI. So much so, in fact, that she enrolled in a graduate degree in Island Studies. She just *needed* to know more about the island she chose to call home. Her thesis focused on telling the stories of Black individuals on PEI through their contributions to the island's food culture.

On PEI, Evelyn has witnessed people put what they've learned in one of her workshops into practice in their community. Islanders' willingness to improve their communities and the amazing results are part of what drives Evelyn to do the work.

"I revel in the opportunity to continue to have conversations about diversity here on the Island..." she wrote for the CBC. "I know that, in time, the changes we all want to see in bettering this community will come to [be]."

GLOSSARY

Words are important to the 2SLGBTQIA+ community.

When a word names how we feel inside about our gender or sexuality, it can make us feel more comfortable with our bodies and our identities. Finding words that represent us can also help us find people like us, our community, and feel less alone. Words are also used to hurt us. Certain words can be used as slurs, words that have negative meanings and are meant to cause us harm. This is why we spend so much time as a community thinking, talking about, debating, and reclaiming or taking back words.

Many words in this glossary have to do with identity, and as such, are highly personal and may be emotionally charged. Each person who uses one of these words to describe who they are and how they feel likely has a different way of defining them. And what is amazing about language, especially language about gender and sexuality, is that it is always changing. It's exciting when our language evolves to better reflect the diversity of the human experience. That also means that by the time you are reading this, the definitions for some of these words may have changed too. That's okay.

The below definitions were drafted by the author. When drafting the definitions having to do with gender and sexuality I referenced the below resources (which are not all geared to youth): *2SLGBTQI Terms and Definitions*, published by Egale; *Queer Terminology from A to Q*, published by QMUNITY, BC's queer resource centre, "The Unicorn Glossary," compiled by Benjamin lee hicks, published in *Teaching Gender and Sexuality at School* by Tara Golstein.

addiction A mental illness that makes a person feel that they need to use drugs or alcohol to survive, function, or feel okay. Another example of an addiction is gambling. When someone is addicted to something they feel that they cannot stop even though it is having a negative impact on their life. People can recover from addiction with medical and/or mental health treatment and support. Each province in Atlantic Canada has addiction treatment services, and other community resources that you can contact if you or someone you know needs help recovering from addiction.

anti-gay discrimination Unfair treatment of gay or queer people based on their sexuality. This can look like denying services or legal rights to gay people that straight people have access to.

asexual A broad identity held by people who experience (or don't experience) various levels of sexual attraction to other people.

biphobia / homophobia / transphobia A dislike or hatred of LGBTQ+ people based on their gender identity, gender expression, or sexuality.

BIPOC: Black, Indigenous, and People of Colour.

bisexual Someone who is attracted to or loves romantically people of more than one gender. Can be shortened to "bi."

chosen family An important concept in the 2SLGBTQIA+ community. It acknowledges that many 2SLGBTQIA+ people are not born into or brought up in families that are also queer and trans, or may not be accepted or supported by those families of origin. Because of this, many 2SLGBTQIA+ people build "chosen family" with other people who either share or accept, support, and celebrate queer and trans identity.

cisgender The term defining people whose gender identity matches society's expectations of the sex they were assigned at birth. So for example, if you were assigned the male sex at birth and your gender identity is male, you would be considered cisgender.

civil rights When referring to the civil rights movement in North America: the fight to end the racial segregation of and discrimination against Black people. That is, the practice of separating people based on their race and denying people of a certain race (Black people) access to services, spaces, or equal treatment. The civil rights movement led to Black people being able to access services and spaces previously only for white people such as schools, certain sections on buses, lunch counters, and pools. Famously, in Nova Scotia, Viola Desmond fought the rule that Black people had to sit at the back of a New Glasgow theatre, away from white people. It led to laws being passed which stopped people from denying others jobs or housing based on their race as well as protecting Black people's right to vote in elections

climate change Changes in the earth's climate, weather, and ecosystems caused by human activity. This includes humans' increased use of substances that produce greenhouse gases that harm the planet, such as oil and gas. Climate change has led to an increase in damaging weather events such as hurricanes, floods, draughts, and forest fires. Many people, especially youth, are taking action to stop or slow climate change by putting pressure on governments and businesses to reduce the harm they are doing to the environment.

closeted/in the closet (*see also* "coming out" / "out") To not share one's gender identity or sexual orientation. Being "in the closet" means to keep your gender identity or sexuality private. People do this for many reasons, including because: it is not safe or comfortable to share it, sharing it could result in being discriminated against, or the person doesn't feel they need to share it.

coming out/out (see also "closeted" / "in the closet") To share your gender identity or sexuality with someone. Also known as "coming out of the closet." No one has to come out, and you should only do so when it is safe and comfortable and with someone you trust. Most people come out multiple times over the course of their lives, to different people, in different situations.

colonial Anything related to a "colony," which refers to a group of people who create a settlement on land that they are not originally from, on behalf of a government or institution.

colonize/decolonize Broadly, to **colonize** means when one country takes land that was not theirs and attempts to control the people who originally lived there, like what was done to Indigenous Peoples in what is now called Canada. This is also called **colonization**. To **decolonize** can mean many things to many people and is widely debated.

Some examples of **decolonization** include: to take apart institutions, laws, and policies enforced by the colonizing government; to foster Indigenous self-governance (that is, Indigenous nations having the power and resources to make decisions about the how they live); to support a return to Indigenous traditional ways; to strengthen people's relationship with—and defend—the environment; return land to the Indigenous Peoples who originally (and still) live there, and much more. Working in this way can also be referred to as **anti-colonial**.

day school Like residential schools, day schools were government and religious institutions that tried to assimilate Indigenous children into (that is, to make them the same as) white European, Christian, Canadian culture. Unlike residential schools, Indigenous children didn't live at the schools. Day school survivors also experienced physical, sexual, and mental abuse.

discrimination/discriminate Treating a person or group of people differently or badly, or denying them rights or services, because of their identity. Discrimination is often based on race, culture, religion, the country someone is from, gender, sexuality, gender identity, or ability/disability (to name a few).

gay Someone who is attracted to or loves romantically people of the same gender as them.

the gay agenda Often used in a humorous way, this term is a response to accusations by people who are against 2SLGBTQIA+ rights and liberation that gay people have plans (or an agenda) to make things "worse." The 2SLGBTQIA+ community has reclaimed this idea of the "gay agenda" to mean the ways they want to make things better, for example: "my gay agenda is to make sure all queer and trans kids feel loved and supported."

gender binary The word "binary" means anything that has two parts or components. "Gender binary" is the false idea that all gender falls into either the category of girl or boy, woman or man.

genderfluid Someone whose gender can move amongst various gender identities.

gender identity This term refers to how you feel inside about your gender, whether you are a boy, a girl, man or woman, a little bit of both, neither, or more! **Gender expression** is how you outwardly present that gender.

gender binary The word "binary" means anything that has two parts or components. "Gender binary" is the false idea that all gender falls into either the category of girl or boy, woman or man.

grassroots Often used to describe the people at a local level (roots) of a community or political movement.

heterosexual Someone who is attracted to, or loves romantically, people of a different gender than their own exclusively. This is also referred to as "straight."

HIV/AIDS Human immunodeficiency virus. According to Canadian HIV & AIDS organization CATIE "HIV can weaken a person's immune system, the body's built-in defence against disease and illness." Spread through bodily fluids shared during unprotected sexual activity or blood. Not spread through touching, kissing, sharing food or drink, sharing a toilet seat, for example. CATIE continues "with treatment and care, people with HIV can live long and healthy lives. HIV treatment also helps prevent HIV transmission to other people." When a person with HIV is not treated medically, it can advance to AIDS (acquired immune deficiency syndrome) and result in severe sickness or death. This was more common in North America in the years before there was medical treatment (the 1980s and early 90s).

homophobia (see **biphobia/homophobia/transphobia**)

Indigiqueer A term used by some Indigenous 2SLGBTQIA+ people to describe their gender identity or sexual orientation. It acknowledges the intersections of queer and Indigenous identities. It can be used instead of or in addition to two-spirit.

intergenerational trauma Mental (also known as psychological) distress experienced by the children, family members, and others who have close relationships with survivors of violence. For example, intergenerational trauma is often experienced by children of people who have survived genocide (attempts by a government to eliminate a certain group of people and their culture), war, and the residential school system in Canada. The symptoms of this trauma can appear as depression and anxiety, family violence, addiction, and more. Healing is possible, and mental health supports are available for those dealing with intergenerational trauma.

intersex An umbrella term for people born with internal and external sex traits—such as genitals, body parts, and/or body chemistry—that fall outside of the male and female binary. According to interACT, Advocates for Intersex Youth, intersex is "a natural variation in human biology, not a medical 'disorder,' and can be identified at birth, during puberty, or later in life."

in the closet (*see* **"closeted"**)

intersectionality How people's different identities, such a race or gender, meet or overlap, and impact their lives.

Inuk The singular of Inuit, the name for the Indigenous people of the Northern or Arctic regions of Canada (including Labrador), Alaska, and Greenland. An Inuktitut word, Inuit translates to "the people."

lesbian Women or non-binary people who are attracted to or love women romantically. (Traditionally the term has been most used by and for women. The definition has been expanded to acknowledge, in part, that lesbian identity has long included gender nonconforming people who may not identify as women.)

marginalized To be on the margins – that is, the edge, away from the centre of power – of a society. When those in power deny power, money, and other resources to a group of people based on their identity, culture, or history. For example, those who live in poverty (without enough money to meet their basic needs) would be considered marginalized. Marginalized people can take their power back when they work together to fight for change.

occupation When a country or government tries to take (occupy) land that is not theirs and control the people who live there and/or have lived there all along. Done in a violent way.

pansexual Someone who is attracted to and may date or be in a romantic relationship with people of various genders.

pathologize(d) To treat something as mentally abnormal or as a disease. Gayness, queerness, and transness have all been pathologized and continue to be pathologized in some places/situations.

policy An official document of guiding principles (or ideas) related to a particular issue. Often used by governments to guide what they do and don't do.

queer An umbrella term for someone who is attracted to people of the same gender, or many genders; defines their gender as being outside of binary gender norms (see the next page for a definition of "gender binary"); and/or identifies as belonging to the 2SLGBTQIA+ community (sometimes called the "rainbow community").

queering To take a thing, idea, or word that was not originally queer and examine, make, or present it in a way that challenges mainstream ideas around gender and sexuality.

residential school Government and religious institutions that tried to assimilate Indigenous children into (that is, to make them the same as) white European, Christian, Canadian culture in the 1800s and 1900s. This meant violently separating Indigenous children from their families, communities, cultures, and languages. Students were subjected to physical, sexual, and emotional abuse by staff. Some children went missing or died at these institutions. As a result, many of the children who attended developed post-traumatic stress disorder (PTSD), and this trauma has also had long-lasting impacts on their families and communities (also known as intergenerational trauma). Learn more about residential schools, and the process of truth and reconciliation, at nctr.ca. Find information about supports for survivors and their families at nctr.ca/contact/survivors/.

sexual orientation Who you are interested in or attracted to romantically. Who you want to date, who you want to kiss, and who you love (as more than a friend).

sober (*also* **sobriety**) A term for not drinking alcohol or taking drugs.

stigmatize to view, describe, or treat something, such as a characteristic of a group of people, in a strongly negative way.

transition Broadly, to change or shift. In relation to gender identity and expression it can refer to a process where a trans or gender diverse person changes their gender expression and body to match their gender identity. This can include changing their name, pronouns, clothing, hair, makeup, way they speak, legal documents, identification (IDs), and more. It can (but does not need to) include taking medications or hormones or having medical procedures that change their bodies to better align with their gender identity. Everyone's transition is different, and it can be an ongoing process. There is no right or wrong way to transition.

transfeminine An umbrella term for a trans person (trans being short for transgender) whose gender identity or gender expression is feminine. What is considered feminine can vary based on someone's culture and upbringing (for example) and is different for everyone. Traditionally, femininity was often defined as characteristics typically associated with women.

transgender Someone whose gender identity does not match society's expectations of the gender associated with the sex they were assigned at birth.

transmasculine An umbrella term for a trans person (trans being short for transgender) whose gender identity and/or gender expression is masculine. What is considered masculine can vary based on someone's culture and upbringing (for example) and is different for everyone. Traditionally, masculinity was often defined as characteristics typically associated with men.

transphobia (see **biphobia/homophobia/transphobia**)

two-spirit (2S) A term for Indigenous people. According to the Wabanaki Two-Spirit Alliance, "two-spirit" refers to "identities that exist outside colonial understandings of gender and sexuality." This can include Indigenous people who also identify as lesbian, gay, bisexual, transgender, queer, Indigiqueer, plus.

undertold Refers to the ignored or hidden histories, stories, and experiences of marginalized groups. Often, these historical experiences happen at the same time as the histories we already understand, but "undertold" stories highlight the cultures and communities that are traditionally left out or missing from the stories we know.

union A labour union is an organization created by workers to fight for good/safe working conditions, fair pay, and benefits such as health insurance.

FURTHER RESOURCES

A selection of some resources that offer support and information to 2SLGBTQIA+ people across the Atlantic Provinces. (Note: Some of these groups serve adults and youth, so some information and services may not be geared towards youth.)

All Atlantic Provinces/National

Kids' Help Phone
Phone: 1-800-668-6868
kidshelpphone.ca

PFLAG (for families of 2SLGBTQIA+ folks)
pflagcanada.ca

Trans Lifeline (youth and adult)
translifeline.org
Phone: 877-330-6366

Wabanaki Two-Spirit Alliance (youth and adult)
w2sa.ca

GSAs
Many schools have Gender and Sexuality Alliances to support 2SLGBTQIA+ students and allies.

Pride Groups (youth and adult)

Many cities, towns, and regions across the Atlantic Provinces also have 2SLGBTQIA+ Pride groups that organize festivals, parades, and events. Search the name of your area (or closest major town or city) plus "Pride" to find them.

New Brunswick

Alter Acadie (youth and adult)
alteracadienb.ca

Chroma New Brunswick (youth and adult)
chromanb.ca

Imprint Youth Association
imprintyouth.ca

Newfoundland and Labrador

The Quadrangle (youth and adult)
thequadnl.com

Trans Youth NL Inc.
transyouthnl.ca

Safe Alliance (HVGB, Labrador) (youth and adult)
Facebook: Safe Alliance

Nova Scotia

Rainbow Refugees (youth and adult)
rainbowrefugeens.com

The Youth Project
youthproject.ns.ca

PEI

P.E.E.R.S. Alliance (youth and adult)
peersalliance.ca

PEI Transgender Network (youth and adult)
peitn.com

ACKNOWLEDGEMENTS

I wrote much of this book while pregnant and then with our baby sleeping in their carrier, strapped to my chest. So, my first thank you needs to be to my tiny co-author, Wynne. Oh, what we've already experienced and accomplished together. My sweet, curious, pensive, and silly (and sometimes spicy) love.

And to my wife, Jill. Thank you for supporting and encouraging me when I thought it would be a good idea to write a book while we were growing our family. Also, for being the best co-mummy to Wynne.

To my family, always. Your support of, pride in, and love for me keeps me going.

I am also very grateful to Whitney Moran, and the team at Nimbus, for their patience with me while I grew and took care of a small human. Thanks for having faith in me and knowing how important a book of 2SLGBTQIA+ possibility models was, especially in our current anti-queer and -trans political climate.

The most fulsome thank you to everyone who is profiled in this book. I truly enjoyed getting to know you, your work, your art, and the impact you've made, through this process. The world was a hard place in 2025; the genocide in Gaza and rise in hateful rhetoric, laws, and violence against 2SLGBTQIA+ people weighed especially heavy on my heart. Your stories were a regular reminder of the strength, resilience, brilliance, creativity, and power of 2SLGBTQIA+ people and community. Especially when we join together for justice, equity, beauty, love, and joy.

My deep gratitude to those featured in these pages who have already passed. For being, so we, too, could be (and hopefully thrive).

Thank you to Lara Lewis for consulting with me about the Mi'kmaw and Indigenous People who should be featured in this book. An extra-special thanks to Evelyn Bradley, Ashley MacIsaac, Veronica Merryfield, and Madonna Doucette for providing insight on some of the complex terms and definitions. The also amazing Jessica McCormick and Sarah Worthman for their Newfoundland and Labrador suggestions. Meredith J. Batt for your New Brunswick knowledge and specifically sending me source material for Hal Hinds's profile. Daniel MacKay for sharing your rolodex of rainbow community members. *Amazing Atlantic Canadian Women* co-author Penelope Jackson for your insights into writing a book in this series.

To all the two-spirit, lesbian, gay, bisexual, trans, queer, intersex, asexual–plus youth, now and future: this book is ultimately for you. I hope it plays a part in

making your life a little brighter and easier. Your mere existence makes this world a better place. Together I know we can make the changes necessary to ensure that every queer and trans youth to come is loved, valued, supported, encouraged, and celebrated.

INDEX

O

P

Q

R

S

T

U

V

W

X

Y

Z

OTHER BOOKS IN THE SERIES

Amazing Atlantic Canadian Kids

ISBN: 978-1-77108-797-1

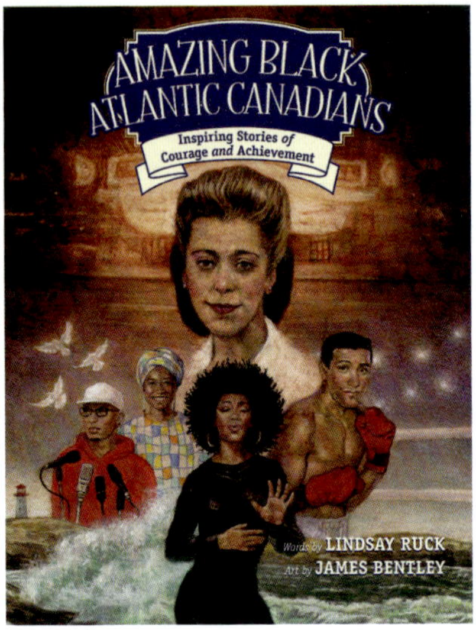

Amazing Black Atlantic Canadians

ISBN: 978-1-77108-917-3

Amazing Atlantic Canadian Women

ISBN: 978-1-77471-016-6

Amazing L'Nu'k

ISBN: 978-1-77471-168-2